Carrington,
*Self-Portrait in Workman's
Cap and Trousers,* 1913.

BLOOMSBURY WOMEN

DISTINCT FIGURES IN LIFE and ART

JAN · MARSH

Foreword by
FRANCES PARTRIDGE

Henry Holt and Company
New York

The author and publisher would like to thank all who have contributed to the making of this book, and most especially to Frances Partridge and Angelica Garnett for generously sharing their memories and pictures; and to Henrietta Garnett, the Charleston Trust, Tony Bradshaw and Sandra Lummis for assistance with illustrations and information. Picture credits and acknowledgements are on page 160.

Henry Holt and Company, Inc.
Publishers since 1866
115 West 18th Street
New York, New York 10011

Henry Holt ® is a registered trademark
of Henry Holt and Company, Inc.

First published in the United States in 1996 by
Henry Holt and Company, Inc.
Published in Canada by Fitzhenry & Whiteside Ltd.,
195 Allstate Parkway, Markham, Ontario L3R 4T8.

Originally published in Great Britain in 1995 by
Pavilion Books Limited.

Library of Congress Catalog Card Number: 95–79117

ISBN 0-8050-4550-3

Henry Holt books are available for special promotions and premiums.
For details contact: Director, Special Markets.

First American Edition—1996

Designed by Janet James
Picture research by Jenny de Gex

Printed in Great Britain
All first editions are printed on acid-free paper. ∞

1   3   5   7   9   10   8   6   4   2

Illustration copyrights are found on page 160

CONTENTS

....

FOREWORD

by FRANCES PARTRIDGE

....

Life stories of the older members of Bloomsbury have been told and retold with a persistence that would have astonished them; their memoirs have been edited and their letters collected, but Jan Marsh has given us something I have never seen before – a comprehensive, impartial and panoramic view of the whole area. We seem to see her flying over Gordon and Tavistock Squares like a bird, and far beyond to Hampstead and Richmond, noting all the activities, relationships and cross-currents of these regions with her wise historian's eye. She has a well-deserved reputation for her books, particularly about women writers and artists, but in this one she feels she is making a firm statement that gender is irrelevant to Bloomsbury. So I was glad to see that though, not surprisingly, her central figures are Vanessa Bell, Virginia Woolf and Dora Carrington, this book gives plenty of room also to the men of Old Bloomsbury – Roger Fry, Maynard Keynes, Lytton Strachey, Leonard Woolf, Duncan Grant and Desmond MacCarthy – even down to the silent Saxon Sydney-Turner, for after all it was among these men that Bloomsbury first saw the light, and it is to their credit that they welcomed the Stephen sisters among them and even allowed Vanessa to dominate.

Nor, evidently, does the 'irrelevance of gender' mean that Jan Marsh is uninterested in the extremely complex and important sexual relationships that flourished in her chosen field. Very far from it; they are as carefully mapped as the London streets in an A to Z guide, and the outer suburbs get full attention. However, I would like to suggest from personal observation that these relationships depended more on love and less on sex than those of today.

Jan Marsh takes us through a period when intelligent young women like Vanessa and Virginia were naturally jealous of the education available to their brothers but not to themselves. Later on we find young men and women sitting on the floor drinking cocoa and eating buns while they talked and argued for all they were worth, with no holds barred. There follows Vanessa's creation of the Friday Club and its stimulating and enjoyable sessions, and soon afterwards came Roger Fry's lectures on Art and the Omega Workshop. 'In fact, Vanessa launched Bloomsbury,' we are told, 'she was clear and determined in her aims.' But the tight collaboration between the friends was inevitably broken by such important events as Vanessa's marriage, motherhood and love-affairs, by the flowering of Virginia's genius and the possibly connected bouts of madness, by the untimely death of Thoby Stephen. But after all we must not forget that these friends didn't think of themselves as a group at that time, but as individuals, each developing more and more outside interests as time went on. The sensitive author has, for instance, noticed that Molly MacCarthy (who first called them 'the Bloomsberries') and her husband Desmond were *original* members while not being exactly central.

This book shows a remarkable talent for summarizing, and is intelligently and lucidly written. Good use is made of quotations from sources. I found only a single point of disagreement – I do not think Carrington was an amateur painter: her Slade career and prizes are not what I am thinking of, so much as the desperate seriousness lying behind her complex attitude to her work.

Writing as someone who knew nearly all of the old guard of Bloomsbury although about twenty years their junior, I have always thought of them with admiration and gratitude mixed with friendship, and their values have influenced me throughout a very long life.

Vanessa Stephen, 1905, at work on her first commission, a portrait of Lady Robert Cecil, seen seated in background.

IN THE
BEGINNING

....

'B loomsbury' was conceived in 1904, when Vanessa and Virginia Stephen and their brothers Thoby and Adrian moved from fashionable Kensington to the quieter London district of Bloomsbury, close to the British Museum. It was born, so to speak, the following year, when the house at 46 Gordon Square became the meeting place for their young artistic and intellectual friends, who gathered on regular weekday evenings to talk and to listen. For the women, this was a new departure – 'sitting up to all hours with young men and saying whatever came first', as Virginia recalled a quarter of a century later.

Virginia was twenty-two and an aspiring writer. Vanessa was twenty-five and already an artist. Together they stitched the social web that bound the Bloomsbury group together. Molly MacCarthy coined the term from her vantage point in Chelsea, and she was also responsible for reconvening the original members of 'old Bloomsbury' in the 1920s, by which time the group had dispersed geographically and acquired a new, younger generation of friends, lovers and artistic associates.

Almost from the start, women were full and equal members – albeit with their own perspective. 'Men and women see the same world but through different eyes,' Virginia was to write later; but over the first few years of Bloomsbury's existence they created a world in which both sexes were able to speak freely on all subjects, including those sexual matters that were otherwise shrouded in genteel prudery or male smoking-room smut. 'We were sexually very free,' recalled Virginia, and 'rather adventurous for those days.' To begin with, however, the sexual freedom was largely conversational

– epitomized by the oft-quoted occasion when Lytton Strachey came into the room, pointed at a stain on Vanessa's white dress, and inquired in his inimitable drawl: 'Semen?'

Could such a thing be said? Virginia was thunderstruck. Then everyone burst out laughing. One of the great Victorian taboos had been broken. From then on sex was a subject of open and often ribald discussion – highly indecent yet in some ways essentially innocent. Virginia did her best to participate, but Vanessa became particularly lewd. She, perhaps, was most determined to escape the world of social convention symbolized by Kensington and her respectable, snobbish relatives. When their Duckworth half-brothers objected that it was morally risky for young women to entertain unchaperoned in Bloomsbury, Vanessa replied with wicked calmness that it was thankfully close to the Foundling Hospital – on whose doorstep illegitimate babies were often deposited – thereby shocking George and Gerald with the kind of joke only men were accustomed to make.

Vanessa launched Bloomsbury. It was she who, after the death of their father, the eminent critic and biographer Sir Leslie Stephen, was responsible for moving the family from Hyde Park Gate – a tall, dark house draped with curtains and gloom – to the light, empty rooms at Gordon Square, where she created sun-filled spaces set off with clean new colours: green and white chintz, Indian paisley shawls thrown over sofas, a red carpet in the dining room. Coalfires burned in the grates, but on at least one occasion matchboxes were banned from the mantelpiece, lest their blue and yellow wrappers clash with the colour scheme. As yet Vanessa's own palette remained somewhat English and dingy, according to the artist Sargent, one of her tutors at the Royal Academy, who urged students to 'get abroad', away from grey-skied Britain, to see colours in sunlight.

At this stage Vanessa was chiefly influenced by Sargent's direct, confident style of painting, so suited to the 'swagger' portrait, which concentrated on tone rather than line and built up pictorial effects with a fluid, well-loaded brush. As she outlined her technique: 'Prepare a canvas with a red ground.

Sketch in the drawing in any neutral colour, then paint quite directly and leave it.' Too many layers or too much re-working, and the picture was liable to lose its freshness, she explained.

At Gordon Square she had her own studio and her first commission to complete, a portrait of Eleanor (Nelly) wife of Lord Robert Cecil. 'Nessa is painting Nelly, who sits now in her own drawing room, by the window, with a green curtain,' noted Virginia in her journal. [Picture 2] The following month, when the portrait was exhibited, she recorded Vanessa's shy triumph:

> A morning devoted to art! – happily, successfully. I went off after breakfast to the New Gallery which might or might not have hung the Nelly picture – and to my great relief found it in the Catalogue and saw it hang fairly in the gallery, which is quite a cheerful beginning. Dashed home, and general rejoicing of a mild description. Went in the afternoon with A[drian] and N[essa] (most unwillingly) to the show again . . .

Though far from confident, Vanessa was clear and determined in her aims, with a firm grasp of artistic identity and integrity that defined her own approach. 'I believe all painting is worth while so long as one honestly expresses one's own ideas,' she told fellow artist Margery Snowden. 'One needn't be a great genius . . . but the moment one imitates other people one's done for. It's allowable while one's a student, learning the language and trying to find out what one does think of it all, but when one once starts alone one must be oneself.'

These wise reflections were not particularly original, she concluded with typical self-disparagement. But they were important. Painting and honest self-expression were the mainstays of Vanessa's life. She attended the two premier art colleges of the day, going on from the Royal Academy schools to study briefly at the Slade School, close to Gordon Square – where the tutor Henry Tonks was wont to observe that women students improved rapidly until their early twenties, when their genius began to tail off as they started to take marriage seriously. Vanessa always took art seriously. 'I should

Vanessa Stephen, Stella Duckworth, Virginia Stephen, mid-1890s. Stella was Julia Stephen's daughter by her first marriage to George Duckworth.

Vanessa Stephen   Stella Duckworth   Virginia Stephen

3

4

LEFT
Henry Lamb,
Portrait of Clive Bell, 1908.

be quite happy living with anyone whom I didn't dislike,' she remarked in 1905, 'if I could paint and lead the kind of life I like.'

Like her mother, the beautiful and saintly Julia Stephen, like Virginia and like their half-sister Stella, Vanessa had large deep-lidded grey eyes, full lips and a grave countenance that suggested serenity in repose. [Picture 3] Her movements were slow and fluid, earning her the childhood nickname Dolphin. But there were volcanoes beneath Vanessa's sedate manner, said Virginia, and although she rarely erupted, her feelings were deep and powerfully warm.

Early in February 1905 Thoby Stephen, who was training to be a lawyer, began inviting his university friends from Cambridge to regular Thursday evening 'at homes', to talk about literature, philosophy, politics. Coffee and biscuits were provided, and when the chairs ran out visitors sat on cushions, as they had done at college. Among the regular visitors were Lytton Strachey, lanky, intellectual, neurasthenic, witty; Desmond MacCarthy, inimitable storyteller and sympathetic, if easily distracted, friend; Morgan Forster, novelist; Maynard Keynes, economist; Saxon Sydney-Turner, silent, music-loving civil servant; and Thoby's closest friend Clive Bell, hearty epicurean with a strong and original liking for French art and literature. [Picture 4]

These serious but often satirical young men, all at the outset of their careers, and their absent friend Leonard Woolf (currently a colonial adminis-trator in the then Ceylon), had been influenced by the Cambridge philo-sopher G. E. Moore, with his ethical rather than religious inquiries into truth and goodness. Moore concluded that the pursuit of 'personal affections and aesthetic enjoyments' – love and art – were by far the greatest good, and this remained a sort of Bloomsbury benchmark, to be discussed and disputed but always respected in matters of moral judgement.

To start with, Thoby's Thursday evenings were largely a masculine affair. Vanessa and Virginia, lacking the university training in philosophical debate, felt slightly marginal amid the abstruse discussions, especially as the young men were unskilled in and indifferent to the niceties of conversation in mixed company. But by the same token, their lack of social graces paid the women the compliment of seriousness. Moore enjoined his disciples never to say anything at all unless they were quite sure it was both true and important.

'They sit silent, absolutely silent, all the time,' noted Virginia when some of Thoby's friends joined a family holiday in Cornwall, reproducing the atmosphere of Gordon Square. 'Occasionally they creep to a corner and chuckle over a Latin joke. Perhaps they are falling in love with Nessa; who knows? It would be a silent and very learned process.'

But intellectual conversation was often animated and provocative. Virginia might mock, but she was stimulated. Later, in *Night and Day*, she attempted to convey the impression of one such gathering:

> One person after another rose, and, as with an ill-balanced axe,
> attempted to hew out his conception of art a little more clearly . . .
> Before long . . . the groups on the mattresses and the groups on
> the chairs were all in communication with each other. . . .
> Katharine turned and smiled.
> 'I wonder what they're making such a noise about?' she said.
> 'The Elizabethans, I suppose.'
> 'No, I don't think it's got anything to do with the Elizabethans.
> There! Didn't you hear them say, "Insurance Bill"?'
> 'I wonder why men always talk about politics?' Mary speculated.
> 'I suppose, if we had votes, we should, too.'

With satire that betrays her own acute envy of male education, Virginia penned a mock review of the delicately titled *Euphrosyne*, a (very) slim volume of verse issued in 1905 by Lytton Strachey, Clive Bell, Saxon Sydney-Turner [Picture 5] and Walter Lamb. 'They entered the College, young & ardent & conceited. . . . They return not less impressed with their own abilities,' she wrote. 'Their most permanent & unqualified admiration is reserved for the works which, unprinted as yet, "unprintable" they proudly give you to understand, repose in the desks of their immediate friends. . . .' But later she wrote, more seriously:

> It filled me with wonder to watch those who were finally left in

the argument, piling stone upon stone, cautiously, accurately, long after it had completely soared above my sight. . . . One had glimpses of something miraculous happening high up in the air. Often we would still be sitting in a circle at two or three in the morning. Still Saxon would be taking his pipe from his mouth as if to speak, and putting it back again without having spoken. At last, rumpling his hair back he wd. pronounce very shortly some absolutely final summing up. The marvellous edifice was complete, one could stumble off to bed feeling that something very important had happened. It had been proved that beauty was – or beauty was not – for I have never been quite sure which – part of a picture.

Not all was so high above her head. In an early story Virginia described the Miss Hibberts of Kensington calling on the Miss Tristrams of Bloomsbury one evening, where people sat on the floor in a smoky room, arguing about a current exhibition. General conversation, the Miss Hibberts found, tended to be scornful of the commonplace, but was always amusing, and amazing when it turned to matters of love and matrimony. Here was Miss Tristram, for instance, 'a young woman of great beauty and an artist of real promise' (perhaps not unlike Vanessa?) frankly discussing marriage with a young man. The way each theorized on the topic was startling, for here love was 'a robust, ingenuous thing which stood out in the daylight, naked and solid, to be tapped or scrutinised as you thought best'.

And often found wanting. In August 1905 Clive Bell, attracted by Vanessa's as yet unawakened sensuousness, her artistic eye and domestic capability, proposed marriage and was refused.

'I was stupid not to see what was going to happen,' she told Margery, 'but even if I had I don't think I should have behaved differently, for I didn't flirt. I might have been less friendly, but that would have been difficult and unpleasant for everyone, and also, unless this particular man is unlike every other, it is highly probable that by this time next year he will have turned to fresh diversions. I can't bring myself to take his unhappiness very seriously. . . .'

Shortly afterwards she was seeking his advice regarding the Friday Club,

Vanessa Bell, *Portrait of Saxon Sydney-Turner*, around 1910.
A member of the Cambridge Apostles and 'Old' Bloomsbury,
Saxon worked in the civil service. 'His friends continued
to believe in him. He was going to be one of the great men
of his time', wrote Virginia with teasing mockery. 'Nothing
was actually published. But "wait a little", his friends said . . .'
An early admirer of Vanessa, Saxon later fell in love with
Barbara Hiles, who married Nicholas Bagenal in a typical
Bloomsbury triangle. Saxon never married.

a group largely composed of painters, set up in conscious emulation of the
Thursday evenings to discuss the fine arts. Her first aim was to hire rooms,
to be used for meetings and small exhibitions, but after looking at prices
and premises she returned to the simpler notion of meeting in private
houses. The chief problem was that of politeness, she wrote:

> We can get to the point of calling each other prigs and adulators
> quite happily when the company is small and select, but it's rather
> a question whether we could do it with a larger number of people
> who might not feel that they were on quite neutral ground. . . .
> It would be much cheaper of course, and we could do with fewer
> members. I should say that we ought to stick to the plan of
> having an occasional exhibition, and for that we should have to
> hire a room specially for a short time.

Though there is no record of the fact, it seems likely that one impulse
behind the Friday Club was the desire to break the male exclusivity of
many artists' meeting places and clubs. Women painters, as Vanessa ironi-
cally noted, were deemed to be 'an especially low breed' and as such were
still denied access to the networks that promoted their male colleagues'
careers. At the time, however, she aspired to create something more akin
to Parisian café society, with its easy informality. Several of her female
friends from the R.A. joined the Friday Club, as did ex-Slade students and
artists like Gwen Darwin and Henry Lamb, drawn in by friendship with
other members of the group. Non-artists were associate or lay members –
including Thoby, Adrian, Saxon Sydney-Turner, Lytton's sister Marjorie
Strachey and her friend Katherine Cox. For a while Clive took up painting
himself, sending two works to the Friday Club's first exhibition in November
1905. The rather mixed membership gave the shows a somewhat indeter-
minate character, half the artists being influenced by Whistler and
Impressionism, according to Virginia, and half remaining staunchly British.

Small exhibitions have such a fugitive existence that it is hard to assess
their impact, but for a decade or so the Friday Club was an established
element in the London art scene, keeping younger painters in touch with

each other's work and helping to maintain the stimulation they had enjoyed at art school, now that all were working in greater isolation. For this Vanessa may take the credit, though she had no desire to lead a coterie and in due course willingly withdrew from the group.

The previous year the Stephens had visited Florence and Venice, where Vanessa discovered that Ruskin's aesthetic theories had little appeal for her. They went on to Paris, where they met up with Clive, visited Rodin's studio and heard of the work of Cézanne, Gauguin, Bonnard and Matisse for the first time. While painters in Britain were still arguing over the Impressionists, French art was already breaking new ground.

In *Jacob's Room*, the novel inspired by Thoby, Virginia drew a thumbnail sketch of a visit to a Paris studio, where avant-garde British artists were working. Jacob commends one picture by his friend Cruttendon. But 'if you'd like to see what I'm after at the present moment,' replies Cruttendon, propping up a second canvas. 'There. That's it. That's more like it. That's. . . .' He squirmed his thumb in a circle round a lamp globe painted white. . . .' Unannounced, Jinny Carslake, 'pale, freckled, morbid', comes into the room. Is she Cruttendon's model, mistress, or fellow painter? She certainly has views on the current canvas. 'It's *that* – that's not right,' she remarks of some feature in the painting under discussion.

Virginia, at this moment, was taking her first tentative steps towards a literary career. Shortly before the move to Gordon Square she had suffered a second serious breakdown in mental health, when she was strictly forbidden to work. But on her return to London she began writing articles and reviews – 'books from *The Times*, the *Academy*, *The Guardian*', she wrote boastfully in November. The following month she published her first review and her first essay, on a visit to the home of the Brontës in Haworth. 'There is nothing remarkable in a mid-Victorian parsonage, though tenanted by genius,' she noted, but the 'three famous ghosts' still seemed to inhabit its rooms; and there is certainly a sense in which Virginia and Vanessa, sisters in shared artistic endeavour, with their own private terms of reference and affectionate competition, measured themselves against those women of genius Charlotte, Emily and Anne Brontë.

Of her own beginnings in fiction she was less assured, writing defensively to a cousin-in-law who had criticized her writing as nebulous and unreal:

> My present feeling is that this vague and dream-like world, without love, or heart, or passion, or sex, is the world I really care about, and find interesting. . . . I wonder if you understand my priggish and immature mind at all? The things I sent you were mere experiments; and I shall never try to put them forward as my finished work. They shall sit in a desk till they are burnt!

Already, it seems, she was innovative, experimental. As girls, Vanessa and Virginia had divided the arts of painting and literature between them. In some ways they were rivals as well as sisters in art: when once Vanessa claimed that painting was more difficult because it involved standing at an easel, Virginia promptly took to writing at a high desk, as in a clerical office. She honed her materials as carefully as Vanessa mixed her colours, writing and re-writing, but at this stage was seldom satisfied that she had achieved the desired effects.

In the summer of 1906 Clive Bell again asked Vanessa to marry him. She replied at length, and with many qualifications, but endeavouring to express her feelings 'quite honestly', saying she knew him too well to dissemble and wished to speak 'naturally and freely'. Though she admitted liking him better than anyone else, she still declined marriage. But clearly Clive had room to hope.

In the meantime the four Stephens laid plans to visit Greece. Thoby and Adrian went ahead, travelling down the Dalmatian coast on horseback and meeting up with Vanessa, Virginia and Violet Dickinson at Olympia. Together they visited ancient sites, where Virginia attempted to reconcile her experiences on the ground with her knowledge of classical Greek literature. Vanessa appreciated the light and landscape, but sadly was sick for much of the trip, confined to hotel bedrooms.

Then when they returned to London Thoby was also ill, with undiagnosed typhoid. He died three weeks later, on 20 November. Two days later, Clive, who had lost his best friend, again asked Vanessa to marry him, and this time she agreed. It perhaps seemed the only way to salvage something of Bloomsbury's (and Thoby's) promise.

Clive was intellectually less high-powered than most of his Cambridge contemporaries. He came from a wealthy family in Wiltshire, whose chief interests were horses and dogs. But he was well-read, a good conversationalist and engagingly sympathetic towards others, especially women. Already adept in the voluptuary arts, he filled his room with armfuls of dark red roses when Vanessa came to dine, in homage to her own limpid qualities. He himself had ginger curls, which soon gave way to baldness, pink cheeks and full lips that could make him look like a petulant cherub. But he was energetic, genial, sociable and keenly self-aware, once describing himself as 'a loiterer in life's pleasant places', and confessing:

> I was made for airy thinking,
> Nimble sallies, champagne-drinking,
> Badinage and argument,
> Reading's infinite content,
> Ill-considered merriment. . . .

They were married in February 1907, and after the honeymoon returned to 46 Gordon Square, where, somewhat shaken, 'Bloomsbury' was re-born in new guise, with Clive taking Thoby's place and Vanessa occupying a central position. Virginia and Adrian moved to a house of their own at 29 Fitzroy Square, just across the Tottenham Court Road. Gordon Square was redecorated and the social conventions were even further loosened – it has been suggested that had Thoby lived, he would have acted as a constraining influence on his siblings in their pursuit of a free and creative lifestyle – by the unconventional habits of the new couple. Once, when Lytton Strachey called, young Mr and Mrs Bell received him from the marital bed. When Leonard Woolf returned from Ceylon, he was exhilarated by the 'sweeping away of formalities' that had occurred among his friends. To have called a (sexual) spade a spade in the presence of Miss Strachey or Miss Stephen would hitherto have been inconceivable, he recalled. Now complete freedom of thought and speech – and use of first names – applied to young women as well as men.

Other things had changed. In the distress of illness and bereavement, several of Thoby's friends as well as Clive had shown themselves to have hearts as well as minds. Over the weeks and months they forged the sort of friendships with Vanessa and Virginia that endure throughout a lifetime: Lytton and Desmond and Saxon were now fixtures in the landscape. This at least partly explains their enduring presence in 'Bloomsbury', for in some respects they were no closer than others who over the years drifted away. Thus, years later, Virginia could write of Saxon:

> His friends continued to believe in him. He was going to be one of the great men of his time. Probably he was working at a poem, after office hours. . . . 'When is it coming out?' they pressed him. 'Anyhow, show us what you've written.' Or was it a history? Or was it a philosophy?. . . . He was studying counterpoint. Also he was teaching himself to paint. He was studying Chinese. . . . Nothing was actually published. But 'wait a little' his friends said. They waited. . . .

Great things were also expected of Lytton, though as yet he too delivered less than he seemed to promise. Having failed to gain a fellowship at Cambridge he lived at home in Kensington, writing constipated articles for the *Spectator* and facetious letters to his friends. But at this moment of crisis he in particular proved a sensitive friend, whose 'great honesty of mind and remorseless poking fun at any sham forced others to be honest too', Vanessa recalled, grateful for the comfort of candour in a time of distress.

Hence, in part, the sexual frankness of early Bloomsbury, which was so shocking for the time (at least in mixed company) and now seems a little juvenile. But there is no doubt that it represented a genuine liberation. The frankness of the studio invaded and combined with the sociability of the drawing room. Wit and laughter, born of friendship, sealed the group identity.

Carrington,
Portrait of E. M. Forster,
1920.
An early associate of
Bloomsbury, Forster's
novels include *A Room with
a View* (1908), *Howard's
End* (1910) and *A Passage
to India* (1924).

BELOW
Gwen Raverat,
*Portrait of
John Maynard Keynes.*
A brilliant economist and
international figure in the
inter-war years, Maynard
Keynes was also one of
the best party-givers in
Bloomsbury.

6

7

8

Vanessa Bell,
Duncan Grant at the Easel,
around 1915.

Nor was this openness confined to heterosexual matters. For their part, the young men were grateful for a social world in which their homosexual feelings were tolerated, accepted as natural, even joked about – but nevertheless kept secure. For it was less than a decade after Oscar Wilde's trial and downfall, and since 1885 such relationships had been illegal; if revealed, they were likely to ruin a career. Once, Vanessa dreamed of Lytton in a vast house of cubicles each containing a young man. 'There was a raid by the police, and each young man was found to have a boy with him,' she told him. 'You were taken in the act and sent to prison, but only for Saturday to Monday, as it was a "first offence." ' A dream perhaps, but an ever-present reality, too. For Lytton Strachey, his cousin Duncan Grant, Morgan Forster and Maynard Keynes were all gay, or 'buggers' in bald Bloomsbury terminology, and all found Bloomsbury a congenial milieu, where sexual orientation was a matter for understanding – and merriment – rather than silence or censure. [Pictures 6, 7, 8]

The Friday Club continued to meet at Gordon Square, where now the pale walls held paintings by Picasso and Vlaminck and where Vanessa planned to hang her studio with mauve and yellow curtains, in a Fauviste manner. The more literary and philosophical Thursday gatherings moved to Fitzroy Square where, according to one observer, Virginia and Adrian resembled an ostrich and a giraffe awkwardly sharing the same enclosure. 'About ten o'clock in the evening people used to appear and come at intervals till twelve o'clock, and it was seldom that the last guest left before two or three,' recalled Duncan Grant. Whisky, cocoa and buns were provided, and talk. Anyone smoking a pipe held out the lighted match to Virginia's dog Hans, who snapped it out. 'Conversation: that was all. Yet many people made a habit of coming, and few who did so will forget those evenings.'

THE ART-QUAKE
OF 1910

....

All unwittingly, the first disruption to this newly created social world was Julian, Clive and Vanessa's first child, born in 1908. He 'came into the world shouting healthily and has continued to do so ever since, whenever he thinks food or attention are due to him', reported Vanessa; and indeed throughout his childhood and youth Julian struck Leonard Woolf as 'roaring and rampageous'. There were servants to cook, clean and take care of the new arrival, so Vanessa was not submerged by domestic matters. But Clive was nervous of the noise, dampness and fragility of babies. One suspects that his nose was somewhat out of joint, for though he never seems to have resented Vanessa's commitment to her painting, in an age when conventionally women gave up careers and independent interests on marriage, he certainly felt displaced by her natural preoccupation with her son. And, rather unforgivably, he turned to his sister-in-law for a restorative flirtation.

Equally unforgivably, Virginia responded. She was feeling bereft, having lost first Thoby and then Vanessa. She envied the warmth of Gordon Square, from which she had been ejected with Adrian, who was no substitute. Both thus unconsciously jealous of Julian, she and Clive combined in guilty pleasures: long walks, long conversations about art and literature, and discreet flattery. Clive could never carry on a conversation with an attractive woman without some show of gallantry, his son Quentin tells us, and Virginia, when stimulated, was an enchanting and even exhilarating companion, as quick-witted as himself, given to inventive flights of fantasy, subversive mockery and penetrating observation. She also liked admiration and despite outward flippancy was somewhat ill at ease with what has been described as Lytton's *cénacle* of university buggers. So Clive's attentions were welcome.

Virginia had begun work on her first novel, later published as *The Voyage Out*. 'The wonderful thing that I looked for is there unmistakably,' replied Clive when presented with the first few chapters; 'one can always recognise it when one gets that glimpse of the thrilling.' He singled out for special praise her power of 'lifting the veil and showing inanimate things in the mystery and beauty of their reality', concluding that it was 'all very exciting and delightful' – as indeed such attention was to Virginia, too.

Vanessa, however, felt doubly excluded and envious. 'I feel painfully incompetent to write letters,' she told her sister, 'and more so as I see the growing strength of the exquisite literary critical atmosphere distilled by you and Clive.' In the autumn she returned to painting, welcoming the company of Henry Lamb, from whom Virginia had commissioned a drawing of her sister. 'We had a long talk about painting, or at least we talked in scraps for a long time, as I was sitting,' she reported. This portrait does not seem to have survived, but around the same time Duncan Grant painted a dark and not very attractive image of Virginia, wearing her hat indoors like a prim Edwardian lady.

Vanessa herself had completed a 'rather ugly but well painted' still life, and begun a similar portrait of Lytton's sister Marjorie, in black with a black hat, leaning forward on the Bells' green sofa, with a jar of yellow chrysanthemums in the background. As Marjorie was certainly 'very ugly', Vanessa was not as nervous of doing her justice as when drawing Virginia.

But now Vanessa found it hard to get to the Friday Club, which met elsewhere, and felt her creative impulses threatened by other duties. She envied her sister's absorption in her novel. 'What wouldn't I give for a steady uninterrupted two months' work?' she wrote from Cornwall, where all she was able to accomplish were 'vague sketches' of Julian, the view from the window and a rather melancholy sunset, which perhaps matched her mood. This year, however, she exhibited at the New English Art Club a still life in cool colours (with a flash of scarlet) called *Iceland Poppies*, which won praise from Sickert. It is composed in triplicates of stripes, vessels and flowers in a manner that, as has been observed, may unconsciously reflect the triangulation of her relationship with Clive and Virginia, and with tonal qualities that suggest her 'introspective, bitter-sweet' and slightly isolated situation.

She was soon pregnant again, her second son, Quentin, being born in August 1910. Despite Bloomsbury's notions of equality, marriage and parenthood were differently experienced by women and men. Another crucial difference, however, was that between women like Vanessa and Virginia who had a clear sense of the importance of their own professional or creative work, and those who did not – a distinction illustrated by the MacCarthys, who were original members of Bloomsbury while not being quite central to it. [Pictures 9, 10]

In January 1906 Desmond proposed to and was accepted by Molly Cornish, who was the same age as Virginia and indirectly related to the Stephens. Her father was provost of Eton College and her mother was a member of the indomitable classes. 'In all disagreeable circumstances remember three things,' she told her daughter. 'I am an Englishwoman; I was born in wedlock; I am on dry land.'

Molly had undefined artistic desires. Of herself when young she wrote: 'My hair is twisted into a Grecian knot; skirts wind about my ankles and hamper me. I am full of vague aspirations and questionings as to what I am to do in life.'

Like everyone else she was charmed off her tree by Desmond's inventive anecdotes and the great novel to rival Tolstoy, Proust and Henry James that he was going to write. Alas, in his case talent was the enemy of promise and Desmond never did more than spin tales – but so delightfully that his friends were always the better for having seen him.

Immediately after their engagement Molly suffered a minor nervous breakdown, apparently caused by fear of the unknown – sex. After their marriage in August 1906 they went to live in the country, where their son Michael and daughter Rachel were born. But Desmond was too often in

RIGHT
Vanessa Bell,
Desmond MacCarthy.
The MacCarthys were
among the oldest
members of the original
Bloomsbury Group.
Molly was responsible for
coining the term 'the
Bloomsberries'.

BELOW
Molly MacCarthy in
1915, from Vanessa Bell's
photograph album.

10

9

RIGHT
Vanessa Bell,
Roger Fry, 1912.
The painting technique
reflects the influence of
French pointillism. Like
Vanessa's picture of
Duncan Grant (no. 8) this
shows Roger Fry at the
easel – a characteristic
pose for the Bloomsbury
artists.

London, leaving Molly isolated and somewhat suspicious of his sociable, sympathetic tendencies. So in 1910 they moved to Chelsea, allowing Molly to be more fully introduced to the alluring yet also intimidating world of Bloomsbury.

'Virginia is delightful and interesting – always rather alarming, but that is fascinating,' she told Desmond bravely, reporting a few months later that they had 'heaps of conversation, abusing the mutual admiration of souls of the young Cambridge'. As this remark suggests, in time Molly herself became a wickedly funny and enjoyable companion, whose inconsequential yet acute observations reduced her companions to tears of laughter.

Unlike either Virginia or Vanessa, however, Molly had no serious projects of her own. 'I am not in the least an artist and find it so difficult to meet the precariousness of life boldly, in the gipsy spirit,' she wrote defensively, ' – so I daren't suggest to Desmond that we should live on air for some years while he writes and writes.' In any case, she concluded perceptively, 'I don't think he would'.

Unlike the Bells, Stephens and Stracheys, the MacCarthys were not well-off. And in considering the social and artistic iconoclasm of the main Bloomsbury women, their secure independent incomes must be given some credit for enabling them to defy convention without descending into impoverished eccentricity. Their financial and intellectual status also allowed them to mix on almost equal terms with all classes, from members of the aristocracy, such as Lady Ottoline Morrell, to miners' sons like D. H. Lawrence, or painters like Mark Gertler, from London's East End. As Frances Partridge remembers, Bloomsbury was conspicuous for its complete freedom from the class consciousness then pervasive in British society.

'The whole show was on the whole a great deal better than any other we have had,' Vanessa told Clive, after visiting the Friday Club exhibition in June 1910. Among the 'most promising' artists was the young Gertler, aged just seventeen, who had two 'rather remarkable' paintings and who she thought was 'going to be good', as indeed it proved.

12

13

ABOVE

On the beach at Studland, Dorset, 1910, from Vanessa's photo album. Vanessa sits with her elder son Julian in an enclosure made of razor-shells, watched by Clive. The seated woman may be Alice Waterlow and the dog possibly Gurth, belonging to Virginia. The perambulator in the background presumably holds Quentin, aged about six weeks. The bathing tent behind Clive reappears in Vanessa's painting of Studland Beach (no. 16).

LEFT

Virginia and Clive at Studland, September 1910. Virginia's hat, scarf and gloves and Clive's jacket, tie and waistcoat indicate that at this date Bloomsbury did not disregard all conventions, even in holiday mode. Later, dress became markedly more casual.

From this same show, however, she actually bought Duncan Grant's *Lemon Gatherers* (now in the Tate Gallery), 'a beautiful composition of women carrying loads on their heads', she told Clive. 'I was very much impressed by it and really think he may be going to be a great painter.'

Bloomsbury was moving into a new phase. The group was expanding with new friends and associates, and a new pictorial world was about to explode before their eyes, with the first Post-Impressionist exhibition in London at the end of 1910, organized by Roger Fry. [Picture 11] In addition to works by Manet, already familiar in Britain, there were thirty-seven pictures by Gauguin, twenty-one by Cézanne (including one *Mont St Victoire*), twenty by Van Gogh (including one *Sunflowers*), and others by Picasso, Matisse, Derain, Rouault, Vlaminck and Maurice Denis.

It was the shock of the new: in Desmond's words 'the Art-Quake of 1910'. The show was hissed and hooted at by the general public and establishment critics, but hailed by the younger generation as a breakthrough. 'Here was a sudden pointing to a possible path, a sudden liberation and encouragement to feel for oneself which were absolutely overwhelming,' Vanessa recalled. 'Perhaps no one but a painter can understand it. . . . But it was as if at last one might say things one had always felt instead of trying to say things that other people told one to feel.'

Manet and the Post-Impressionists certainly liberated painters (and indirectly writers, too) from the constraints of realism, soberness and academicism. In France, the avant-garde painters were known as *les Fauves* — the wild beasts, in contrast to the tame variety. At the cost of painstaking 'finish', the new art embraced expressive colour, line, composition and rhythm. Downgrading 'content', painting concentrated a formal aesthetic where emotion was rendered visually, without sentiment or the need for verbal 'explanation'. A portrait ceased to be a photographic likeness. To its critics, such art was crude, incompetent, vulgar. To its enthusiasts, it offered a whole new way of seeing. Painters did not seek to imitate life, but to find an equivalent for life, Roger Fry declared. The impersonality of objects, colours, shapes cleared away the confusions of literalism. As Vanessa

Vanessa Bell,
Virginia Woolf knitting,
1912.
The same winged
armchair is seen in
Conversation Piece at Asheham
(below).

14

Vanessa Bell, *Conversation
Piece at Asheham*, 1912.
From left: The
exceptionally tall Adrian
Stephen, Leonard Woolf
and Clive Bell, wearing
blue socks.

15

Vanessa Bell, *Studland Beach*, 1912.
'The reduction of form to elemental shapes expresses a
feeling which is often austere and remote, but also
related to her maternal experience', writes Frances
Spalding. The taller straw-hatted figure in the foreground
is thought to be based on Virginia Woolf.

Duncan Grant,
Pamela, 1911.
A study of Roger Fry's
daughter, shown in front
of the lily pond in the
garden of Fry's home near
Guildford.

17

Duncan Grant,
*On the Roof at 34 Brunswick
Square*, 1912.
Adrian Stephen is seated
between Virginia Stephen
and Leonard Woolf, soon
to be married. Painted in
hot weather during the
months that they shared
the Brunswick Square
house with Duncan Grant
and Maynard Keynes.

18

19

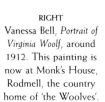

RIGHT
Vanessa Bell, *Portrait of
Virginia Woolf*, around
1912. This painting is
now at Monk's House,
Rodmell, the country
home of 'the Woolves'.

20

explained later, when asked to lecture on painting: 'even a kitchen coal scuttle may become the most exciting continuation of curves and hollows, deep shadows and silver edges, instead of a tiresome thing to be filled with coal.'

But if in retrospect the Post-Impressionist season was a time when everything seemed springing to new life, when 'all was a sizzle of excitement, new relationships, new ideas, different and intense emotions', Vanessa was herself still under stress. Virginia had been ill again, and although the flirtation with Clive had faded, Vanessa was now aware that her husband's philandering also included a mistress of long standing. Combined with anxiety over the new baby, this was aggravated in spring 1911 by a trip to Turkey with Clive, Harry Norton and Roger Fry, during which Vanessa suffered a nervous collapse compounded by an early miscarriage. Roger, whose unremitting energy was often responsible for a certain exhaustion among his fellow travellers, took competent and sensitive care of her. Back in Britain they began a discreet but passionate affair. The liberation of art had some unexpected side-effects.

Roger was a quasi-widower. His wife Helen had tragically lost her sanity and been recently committed to an asylum. Their two children Julian and Pamela were cared for by Roger's sister Margery Fry at his house near Guildford. A relatively recent recruit to Bloomsbury, he was largely responsible for the whole Post-Impressionist project, as critic, painter, collector and propagandist. It was seeing him on a daily basis, listening to him, reading, and talking to him about art, that made Vanessa realize what an enthralling companion had come into her life. 'Our feelings jumped together at each new sight,' she wrote.

'Nessa, I should be a real artist, really truly and without doubt if I could draw you often, because you have this miracle of rhythm in you, and not in your body only but in everything you do,' Roger wrote to her. He loved to look at her as if he were drawing her, running his eyes from her fingertips to the throat that 'swells like a great wave when you throw back your head for me to kiss it'. Under such admiration Vanessa rediscovered her pleasure in love, and regained her sexual confidence – by turns teasing and open, direct and self-contented.

Vanessa's frailty earlier in the year seems to have helped Virginia out of her dependency – or at least shown that she herself could not always depend on her sister, who until now had borne the brunt of Virginia's mental instability, regularly consulting doctors to arrange for her admission to what Quentin Bell, with the bluntness of Bloomsbury, has called 'a polite madhouse for female lunatics', and also helping to find country retreats from the excitement of London.

In 1911 Virginia leased a house in the village of Firle, near Lewes in Sussex, where she persisted with her novel and enjoyed long solitary walks that were to become a lifelong habit. She was still prone to despair as well as mania, writing in June to tell her sister: 'I could not write, & all the devils came out – hairy black ones. To be 29 & unmarried – to be a failure – Childless – insane too, no writer. . . .'

Here, encapsulated, was the dilemma faced by the women of Bloomsbury (and the men, too): how to succeed – at something – and also find love, companionship, parenthood. Art and love remained the twin goals. Ambition was a spur with a sharp edge.

She had some new friends: Katherine (Ka) Cox, who had studied at Cambridge and was a supporter of worthy causes including women's suffrage; [Picture 22] and Ka's friend Rupert Brooke, golden-haired poet, with whom Virginia went to stay, swimming naked in the Granta on a summer night, and who himself stayed overnight at her house in Firle. [Picture 21] Soon afterwards she and Ka joined a camping holiday in Devon with Rupert and the Olivier sisters, lovers of the simple life. This group, who also included Gwen and Jacques Raverat, were nicknamed the 'Neo-Pagans' by Virginia, in reference to their lifestyle. Bloomsbury in general did not take to tents; however spartan their style, they preferred a roof over their heads on any country holiday.

Ka Cox proved a staunch friend to Virginia during her worst periods of breakdown, and although never more than on the fringe of Bloomsbury by

21

ABOVE
Virginia Woolf with Rupert Brooke, at a 'Neo-Pagan'
summer camp on the edge of Dartmoor, 1911. Other
campers included Brynhild and Noel Olivier, James
Strachey and Maynard Keynes, who wrote: 'The hard
ground, a morning bathe, and no chairs, don't make one
nearly so ill as one would suppose.' Earlier in the year
Virginia had visited Rupert in Grantchester. He was also
invited to Asheham, where he saw 'Old Nessa' sitting
on the floor in a blue skirt and emerald green sweater,
piecing together an Omega table-top. Brooke died on
active service in 1915, having written the famous lines
'If I should die, think only this of me . . .'

RIGHT
Duncan Grant, *Study of Ka Cox*, 1913.
Katherine (Ka) Cox nursed Virginia during her 1913
breakdown. Unhappily in love with Rupert Brooke, she
eventually married painter Will Arnold Forster.

virtue of this friendship, she did sit for Duncan Grant for more than one Post-Impressionist portrait, wearing her characteristic headscarf. The image is striking – an expressive likeness conveying much of Ka's solidity and strength, even while the surface is broken into myriad planes in an almost Cubist manner.

As her despairing remark to Vanessa makes plain, Virginia was worried about marriage. 'These June nights – how amorous they make one,' she had added. Two years earlier Lytton Strachey had precipitately proposed, and been accepted; he was one man whom Virginia admired intellectually and did not feel threatened by. But the next day Lytton realized it was impossible: his inclinations were wholly homosexual. Simultaneously Virginia backed off too, and the incident was quickly cancelled. Proposals from other suitors followed, but none to which she responded with any true desire. In July 1911 she discussed the question rather dispassionately with one admirer, who observed that in Bloomsbury she inhabited a hornets' nest of emotional intrigue, and inquired pathetically (but also prudently) whether she would flirt when married. Not if she were in love with her husband, replied Virginia, which evidently scared off this suitor.

In the autumn she and Adrian leased a new house, at 38 Brunswick Square, which they shared with Duncan Grant and Maynard Keynes. Meals were provided on trays by the cook-housekeeper, according to requests posted each morning. Here, on his return from Ceylon, Leonard Woolf also lodged, and here, the following summer, Duncan painted his co-residents sunning themselves on the roof, in a pointillist manner. [Picture 18] By January 1912 Leonard knew he was in love with Virginia. 'Before this week I always intended not to tell you unless I felt sure you were in love & would marry me,' he wrote to her. But Virginia was not certain: she felt no physical attraction towards Leonard and had a deeply neurotic fear of her own sexuality. A curious Bloomsburyish courtship followed, with attempts at rational analysis on both sides. 'I began life with a tremendous, absurd, ideal of marriage,' she wrote, in reference to her parents. Then, her

23

LEFT
Vanessa Bell and Molly
MacCarthy posing in
Vanessa's studio in
Gordon Square, around
1914.

BELOW
Roger Fry, oil sketches of
Vanessa Bell, around 1913.

24

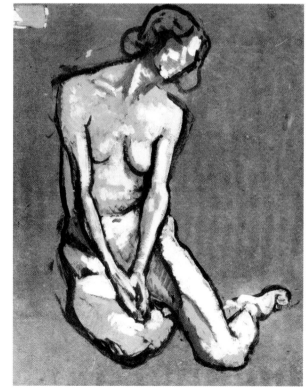

25

Vanessa arranging a vase of flowers at Asheham
around 1912, with Duncan Grant. Both artists regularly
produced flower and still-life paintings.

observation of many unions made her disgusted. But 'now I only ask for someone to make me vehement, and then I'll marry them!'

For all his cool Cambridge intellectuality, Leonard proved vehement and determined. 'You may be vain, an egoist, untruthful as you say, but they are nothing compared to your other qualities – magnificence, intelligence, wit, beauty, directness,' he wrote. And in May he resigned from the Colonial Service, burning his bridges in an eloquent willingness to sacrifice all for love. On 29 May Virginia agreed to marriage, and the wedding took place on 12 August, followed by a long honeymoon in Europe.

Earlier in the year she had exchanged the house at Firle for a more isolated farmhouse not far away at Asheham, which she shared with Vanessa. This became the first country outpost of Bloomsbury and ever after retained their affection, despite its sunless location and incurable tendency to creak and groan in the night as if possessed by ghosts. 'Wandering through the house, opening the windows, whispering not to wake us, the ghostly couple seek their joy,' wrote Virginia in *A Haunted House*:

> 'Here we slept,' he says. And he adds, 'Kisses without number.' 'Waking in the morning –' 'Silver between the trees –' 'Upstairs –' 'In the garden –' 'when summer came –' 'In winter snowtime –' The doors go shutting far in the distance, gently knocking like the pulse of a heart.'

Here, at Asheham, Lytton sat in a deckchair to be painted by Vanessa, Roger and Duncan. Here Vanessa painted while Clive and Roger planned the second Post-Impressionist show, to include contemporary British painters. 'As it has been so cold Duncan and I have been painting still lives indoors – servants brought in flowers from the garden,' she wrote to Roger. 'I find that I am not now much impeded by working with Duncan although of course I always think why didn't I see it like that?' [Picture 26]

Her *Nosegay*, exhibited with the 1912 Post-Impressionists, may have been painted from the Asheham flowers. Certainly her striking view of the house behind a plump haystack, also exhibited, has a solidity that contrasts with Duncan's more playful works at this period and shows her own distinct style. As she told Margery Snowden, her current works reflected 'no one's ideas but my own'. Nevertheless, as her participation in the second Post-Impressionist show indicates, she was among the few British artists to follow and absorb the Modernist influence, and for a while, under the influence of Braque and Picasso, she deployed Cubist techniques, experimenting with radical new ways of painting.

Visitors flowed and ebbed at Asheham this season, as Vanessa strove to furnish the house and create a garden. Duncan came for a weekend and stayed a fortnight. Maynard appeared; so at intervals did Roger and Clive, and two young artist friends of Duncan, Frederick Etchells and his sister Jessie, whom Vanessa sketched painting in the Asheham studio, Fred at the easel and Jessie on the floor with a drawing board. [Picture 29]

Molly MacCarthy also arrived, primarily to see Clive, who was pursuing her. Though amusing and original, Molly did not share Bloomsbury's liking for bold and bawdy talk. 'She is we all thought very nice,' reported Duncan to Virginia, 'but it was rather a strain on our tongues which had wagged rather free before.' She and Vanessa discussed marriage, Molly admiring Vanessa's freedom but still in thrall to conventional views of love, deceit and betrayal. Nevertheless, she plucked up courage and despite her misgivings embarked on an affair with Clive. She didn't know why they were such friends, she had told him a few weeks earlier, as she couldn't look at a picture for more than a minute without yawning. But he was kind as well as flattering, and so full of energy. 'Clive's great merit of vitality is so pleasant,' she wrote on a later visit to Asheham, adding that the laid-back atmosphere suited her. Her fellow guests all seemed utterly irresponsible and lazy, except Vanessa and Duncan who worked away at 'mysteriously bad daubs of genius'.

Clive's attentions also helped Molly come to terms with Desmond's inadequacies (he had, he confessed later, decided at seventeen to capitalize on being incapable, as 'incapable people always have things done for them'). Molly feared she would be turned into a morose, naggish, peevish, lonely woman, disillusioned and disappointed by Desmond's failure, and their children (now three in number) would wonder why he didn't provide a

better life 'as other fathers do who have made careers or have honours if not wealth'. Reading between the lines, the affair with Clive determined Molly on her own course of irresponsibility, trading like Desmond on wit, originality and the eccentric charm that became the MacCarthy hallmark, and in doing so brightening others' lives as well as her own.

She also loosened her inhibitions, as a nude photo of her and Vanessa in the studio at Gordon Square suggests. Under Vanessa's leadership, such unembarrassed nudity – to which artists were of course already accustomed in the studio and life class – became a Bloomsbury feature in private and sometimes in public: Vanessa and Virginia appeared together as bare-shouldered, bare-legged Tahitian girls out of Gauguin at one Post-Impressionist party; at another, Vanessa danced topless. Her children were among the first generation to run naked in summer. [Pictures 23, 24, 25]

The previous year Vanessa had painted *The Bathers*, a figure composition based on a seaside scene at Studland in Dorset where she, Roger and other friends were holidaying. [Pictures 12, 13] Like Duncan's *Bathers*, this was indebted to Maurice Denis's *Grandes Baigneuses*, on show at the 1910 exhibition. One reclining figure in a straw hat is said to be drawn from Virginia, and two of the children based on Julian and Pamela Fry. This was the forerunner to the far more innovative *Studland Beach*, completed the following year, in which the figures are rendered as anonymous groups of women and children, reduced in form to elemental shapes held in tension by their diagonal positioning and the tall beach tent. [Picture 16]

According to Vanessa's biographer, this work marked a radical advance in artistic terms, striding away from mimetic representation towards simplification and even abstraction. It expressed an emotion that is often austere and remote, writes Frances Spalding, but was also related to the artist's maternal experience. Both here and in two subsequent works on a monumental scale that are now lost – a six-foot *Nativity* for Roger's house near Guildford, and a similar-sized canvas of a woman and child on a bed –

Vanessa endeavoured to convey the depth of her feeling about motherhood without recourse to anecdote or sentimentality.

The transition in style and representation is visible in *Nursery Tea*, depicting women and children around a table, in an abstracted composition held together by diagonal tension and areas of vivid colour, with something of a child's eye view or Polaroid snapshot effect about the perspective. 'I am just in an exciting stage as I flatter myself that I am painting in an entirely new way,' Vanessa told Roger as she worked on this canvas in June 1912. [Picture 27] 'I am trying to paint as if I were mosaicing – not by painting in spots, but by considering the picture as patches.' At the same time, the red-haired child is unmistakably Quentin, and the other almost certainly Julian Fry. From a blend of formal severity and personal feeling, the artist has succeeded in replacing anecdote with essence, in a unique expression of what painting meant to her.

The aim was simplification of forms and denial of detail. As Vanessa explained to Leonard, who held more traditional views: 'It is clearly possible to use imitation or representation in producing a great work of art, but it can't be the object of a great artist to tell you the facts at the cost of telling you what he feels about them . . . the reason that artists paint life and not patterns is that certain qualities in life, what I call movement, mass, weight, have aesthetic value'.

These major works represent a real departure, a landmark in British art as well as in Vanessa's own development. They can be seen as the visual equivalent of T. S. Eliot's early poem *The Love Song of J. Alfred Prufrock*, first published in 1915. The same impulse was responsible for Vanessa's portraits of Virginia done in this period, notable for the erasure of features and the clarity of posture: as has been said, the figures are faceless, yet immediately recognizable; even more vividly than photos, these images convey the presence of their sitter, as she sits knitting, in the same wingchair as is seen in the earlier *Conversation Piece*. [Pictures 14, 15] And this productive phase in Vanessa's career was marked by the beginning of an all-female *Conversation*, sometimes known as *Three Women*, which she started in 1913 and completed in 1918. 'I think you are a most remarkable painter,' wrote Virginia on seeing this, maintaining that in paint Vanessa was also 'a short story writer of great wit' in a way that roused her own envy. 'I wonder if I could write the *Three Women* in prose.'

The Post-Impressionist impact on literature was felt later than its impact on art. But as Virginia wrote subsequently in her biography of Roger, 'Cézanne and Picasso had shown the way; writers should fling representation to the winds and follow suit.' Sentences were like brushstrokes, with their own rhythm and line distinctive to the writer.

At first she was envious. 'Artists are an abominable race,' she complained to Violet Dickinson as the 1912 exhibition drew to its close. 'The furious excitement of these people all over the winter over their pieces of canvas coloured green or blue, is odious.' But she had already discussed colour with Vanessa, who professed herself unable to understand how writers could convey shades: 'the mere words gold or yellow or grey mean nothing to me, unless I can see the exact quality of the colours,' she wrote.

In response, Virginia's fiction became visual, impressionistic, avoiding narrative ('every picture tells a story' had been the Victorian maxim) in favour of expressive word-painting. In *Three Women*, the curving lines of the figures lead the eye to the central flowers, enclosed by curtains. So in *Kew Gardens*, begun by Virginia in 1917, the eye and ear are focused on a moment:

> Yellow and black, pink and snow-white, shapes of all these colours, men, women and children, were spotted for a second upon the horizon, and then, seeing the breadth of yellow that lay upon the grass, they wavered and sought shade beneath the trees, dissolving like drops of water in the yellow and green atmosphere, staining it faintly with red and blue. It seemed as if all gross and heavy bodies had sunk down in the heat motionless and lay huddled on the ground, but their voices went wavering from them as if they were flames lolling from the thick waxen bodies of candles. Voices, yes, voices, wordless voices, breaking the silence suddenly with such depth of contentment, such of desire, or, in the voices of children, such freshness of surprise;

breaking the silence? But there was no silence; all the time the motor omnibuses were turning their wheels and changing their gear; like a vast nest of Chinese boxes all of wrought steel turning ceaselessly and indifferent, shaking space ceaselessly one within another, the city murmured; on the top of which the voices cried aloud and the petals of myriads of flowers flashed their colours into the air.

As in art, there were new departures in prose.

Vanessa Bell, *Nursery Tea*, 1912. 'I am just at an exciting stage because I flatter myself I am painting in an entirely new way,' she wrote.

27

OMEGA
AND OTTOLINE

....

'Every piece of furniture was painted with primitive sketches of human figures, or of flowers, or of vessels, or of animals. On the front of the mantelpiece were perversely but brilliantly depicted . . . two nude, crouching women who gazed longingly at each other across the semi-circular abyss of the fireplace . . .' Thus Arnold Bennett in his novel *The Pretty Lady* described a typical decorative scheme in Bloomsbury, evidently derived from the interior of a house belonging to a client of the Omega Workshops – the next Bloomsbury creation.

Roger Fry dreamed up the Omega Workshops in 1912, inspired partly by Post-Impressionist colour and line, partly by the atelier run by Parisian designer Paul Poiret and partly, one suspects, by his love for Vanessa and their shared pleasure in joint artistic projects. 'What wouldn't I give to be helping you decorate the room,' she told Roger in summer 1911. 'I believe you do have an extraordinary effect on other people's work – I always feel it when I'm with you.' She herself had already decorated and furnished Virginia's villa at Firle with 'patches of Post-Impressionist colour', and later this year she did a mural design of two monumental figures for a tall chimneybreast at Durbins, Roger's home in Surrey.

Both were attracted to the decorative and popular arts of the Mediterranean [Picture 37] – in time Bloomsbury built up a great collection of pots and plates from Italy, Spain and Greece – and early in 1912 they were thinking of getting together a group of artists to put their design ideas into practice. 'It is time the spirit of fun was introduced into furniture and fabrics,' Roger declared later, placing the impulse firmly in the wake of the second Post-Impressionist show:

> With the appearance of the new Cézannian art in England, most of all with the first sight of Gauguin's intensely decorative silhouettes, the younger English artists began at once to practise design in such a way that made them again fit to take a hand in the applied arts.

With Duncan and two other male artists, Roger had enjoyed painting murals for the Borough Polytechnic in London. For a decorative scheme planned for Newnham College Cambridge (never executed but presumably meant to celebrate wise or illustrious women) Duncan had also painted his pointillist Queen of Sheba. [Picture 28] According to Vanessa, this was 'too sweet, too pretty and too small'. She herself longed to work on a large scale and produce yards and yards of 'bold and piquant fabrics', as well as the playful painted boxes she was decorating.

At the Grafton Group show in March 1913 she exhibited a screen painted with daffodils. Shortly afterwards she and Roger went to Italy with Clive and Duncan to study frescoes and mosaics. On their return the Omega Workshops was launched, as a limited company with capital provided by Bells and Frys. Roger, Vanessa and Duncan were co-directors. It was, Roger explained, a workshop for decorative and applied art, employing young artists whose painting showed strong decorative feeling and who 'will be glad to use their talents on applied art both as a means of livelihood and as an advantage to their work as painters and sculptors'. In June Vanessa proposed an inaugural dinner for Roger, to be given by all the grateful artists and to which potential clients would be invited. After dinner all would repair to the Omega shop in Fitzroy Square, with its painted furniture and painted walls. 'There we should all get drunk and dance and kiss, orders would flow in and the aristocrats would feel sure they were really in the thick of things,' she wrote .

It was the gaiety of the Omega work that most pleased the *Times* critic

28

LEFT
Duncan Grant, *The Queen of Sheba*, 1912. It is said that the figure of King Solomon was inspired by Lytton Strachey and that of the Queen by his sister Pernel Strachey, principal of Newnham College, Cambridge and a pioneer of women's learning.

29

Vanessa Bell, *Jessie and Frederick Etchells in the Studio*, 1912. Painted at Asheham. Both Jessie and her brother Fred were involved in the Omega Workshops. The relative status of male and female artists at this date seems to be reflected in their positions here – Fred standing at the easel, Jessie with drawing board on the floor.

at the press launch. The artists seemed to have enjoyed what they were doing, even if some of the tables looked like ordinary tables painted 'in an irrational manner'. The bedspreads, parasols, fabrics and wallpapers were more innovative, he added, and one dress design succeeded in being both novel and fashionable.

Earlier in the year Clive, following Roger's ideas, had articulated the idea of 'significant form' as the basis for all good art. What quality was common to the windows of Chartres, Mexican sculpture, a Persian bowl, Chinese carpets, Giotto's frescoes, Poussin, Cézanne, and Matisse? he asked. 'Only one answer seems possible – significant form.' Or – as Roger joked to the press – 'significant deformity', for this was a notion that demoted the representational fidelity of Victorian painting, introducing ideas of abstraction to art and also bringing the design arts into closer relation with painting and sculpture. Omega designs were thus influenced by a wide range of sources, from Italian earthenware to Picasso's drawings, textiles for African markets and the phenomenally popular Ballets Russes, which had taken London and Paris by storm. Coincidentally but significantly, the Omega opened its doors on the same day as both the ballet *Ivan the Terrible* and Irving Berlin's *Hello Ragtime!*, two musical sensations of the season. The movement and rhythm of dance and popular music were often incorporated into Omega art, sometimes as stylized, athletic figures, sometimes as theatrical backdrops.

According to the *Daily News* reporter, 'the walls of the Post-Impressionist home will not be as the walls of the ordinary home. I saw an example in which the walls were covered with a wonderful landscape [of] pale purple skies, and shining moon, and blue mountains.' Bold colours, broad forms, loose brushwork: all combined to eliminate the ornate Edwardian style of interior decorations, without falling into the folksiness of Arts and Crafts or 'Garden Suburb' design.

'It is time the spirit of fun was introduced into furniture and fabrics,' Roger insisted. And if people grew tired of one scheme, they could easily have another: speed, spontaneity and liveliness were the Omega hallmarks.

This chair was witty, conversational, he explained to a doubtful newspaper-man, with its blue and green seat and blue and yellow legs – far more amusing than an ordinary chair.

Production began in earnest (if that is the word) in summer 1913. Roger, Vanessa and Duncan were the chief designers. Others included the artists Wyndham Lewis and Fred Etchells, while production workers were recruited from younger and mainly female artists including Jessie Etchells, Winifred Gill, and ex-Slade students Barbara Hiles and Dora Carrington, together with Gladys Hynes and Nina Hamnett. Each was employed for a maximum of three half-days per week, so as not to encroach on their painting time, and the generous rate of pay – ten shillings per session – freed most from financial anxieties.

Omega designs were faithfully but not mechanically executed, in order to retain the freshness of hand-painted items, sometimes achieved at the cost of true professionalism and finish. According to Roger, Omega artists worked 'with the object of allowing free play to the delight in creation on the making of objects for common use. They refuse to spoil the expressive quality of their work by sand-papering it down to shop finish, in the belief that the public has at last seen through the humbug of the machine-made imitation of works of art.' But inevitably, this led to problems with professional techniques such as waxing, varnishing, and painting of textiles. 'Naturally, the chairs we sold stuck to people's trousers,' said Lewis with typical exaggeration.

The workroom was upstairs. Here, Winifred remembered, they painted cushions, scarves and lampshades in dyes on silk prepared by being brushed with size and afterwards sent out for 'fixing'. 'We only copied our own designs with the single exception of a design of Vanessa's (for a lampshade) which had to be repeated in all sizes.' They also painted table legs, and trays. 'O yes and endless candlesticks. When I remember Nina Hamnett at work it is always with a candlestick in her hand.' In fact, these seem to have been the stems of tall table lamps, each painted geometrically, to be topped by a matching shade; but the term reminds us that at this date not all households were supplied with electric light.

Jessie Etchells made up bracelets of brightly coloured beads. She was an accomplished artist, dreamy in temperament, with pale gold hair and milk-white skin. Once, Winifred remembered, Jessie said how terrible it must be to grow old and see desire fade from the eyes of men – to which Winifred retorted: 'Wouldn't trouble me. I've never seen it there.'

In the autumn of 1913 the Omega was invited to showcase its work at the Ideal Home exhibition. Vanessa, Duncan and Roger each did a large wall panel, six feet high, covered with dancing figures in green and ochre, red pilasters between and a blue dado below. It was great fun working on such a large scale, Vanessa reported to Clive. Painted chairs, tables, lamp-shades and striking fabrics in yellow and brown completed the effect, remarkably preserved for posterity in an early colour photograph. [Picture 41]

Not unexpectedly, Etchells and Lewis (justly described by Leonard Woolf as a 'bilious and cantankerous' man) soon defected from the enterprise, leaving the partners with an increased workload. One of Vanessa's first Omega productions was a folding screen (English houses at this date being draughty and often bathroomless, screens were much in demand for warmth and privacy around a movable bath tub) based on an unfinished painting of a summer camp she had joined in Norfolk, showing a threefold scene of figures and tents and demonstrating the interchangeability of design and easel art. [Picture 42]

Because they were not made to last, few Omega interiors survive, and most of the objects now have a rather battered look, so it is difficult to get a firm impression of the original boldness of the style. Charleston farmhouse, the most complete surviving Bloomsbury interior, retains some Omega traces but these are overlaid with later, softer, and rather whimsical forms; Omega itself was more geometric and abstract, tending also to unusual colour combinations erroneously described as garish but certainly seldom seen in interior design. A favourite Omega colour was a warm mulberry, mixed from Venetian red, black and white pigments, always associated with Vanessa by Winifred Gill, as she recalled the 'all-out effort' to get the showroom open, with the back wall distempered in pale puce and stencilled with large leaf sprays in spattered dark purple.

For Christmas Vanessa, who had previously decorated the boys' bedroom at Gordon Square with vigorous zebras and jaguars, designed a whole nursery room for the workshop, painted by her and Winifred. The floor was covered with brilliant yellow felt, to match the curtains; the ceiling had stylized clouds; and on the walls was a landscape 'expressed with some freedom' according to the *Observer*'s critic, with a blue ribbon representing mountains, a pale blob for a lake and unmistakably, on the stretch of yellow that stood for sand, the black silhouette of a huge elephant. The effect was completed with painted furniture, Omega rugs and large wooden animals on wheels.

Early in 1914 Vanessa was in Paris, with Roger and Clive and Molly. Gertrude Stein took them to Picasso's studio and they also visited Matisse and Derain. Picasso was one of the greatest geniuses, Vanessa told Duncan, and the French artists' current work had a discernible effect on Omega productions. On her return to London Duncan sent a basket of oranges and lemons, which were so lovely that she at once put them into a yellow Italian pot for a still life, despite 'all modern theories – I mean one isn't supposed nowadays to paint what one thinks beautiful. But the colour was so exciting.' She then took the rest of the fruit round to the Omega, certain that Roger would find them equally so.

To Roger's dismay, Vanessa had fallen in love with Duncan, whose artistic gifts and gentle temperament attracted her in equal measure. Despite his devotion, Roger had proved a demanding partner, while his own painting remained too stolid and even costive for her taste – and Vanessa was not sufficiently liberated from conventional notions of gender to be comfortable with loving someone whose talent was inferior to her own. They remained close friends and colleagues, however, and this spring visited a commercial pottery together to try their hand at throwing clay, with a view to Omega producing its own ceramics. It was most exciting, she reported to Duncan. 'Of course one couldn't possibly do anything big yet . . . but the feeling of the clay rising between one's fingers is like the keenest sexual joy! You *must* come and do it soon.' Plans were laid to decorate jugs, bowls and vases in typical Omega style. The most notable was a black dinner service, which naturally aroused press mockery. 'Imagine how perfectly gorgeous tomato soup would look in a black soup tureen!' exclaimed one newspaper; 'and the plates are obviously waiting for salad – vivid green lettuce, shy radishes and magenta beetroots! Fruit would be a Futurist feast in those black bowls. . . .'

Vanessa was also responsible for Omega's forays into fashion, with the making up of dresses and cloaks in Omega fabrics, which she hoped would reflect current style and yet not look like regular dressmakers' garments. On occasion, Winifred and Nina modelled Omega fashions; in the photograph shown Nina is wearing an oyster-coloured satin evening cloak painted in greens and browns. [Picture 30]

Nina Hamnett was a recent and as it turned out a temporary recruit to the Bloomsbury art world. Born in west Wales in 1890, she trained at Frank Brangwyn's London School of Art and made her exhibition debut in 1911. In 1912 she visited Paris, bobbed her hair and painted a self-portrait wearing a wide-brimmed hat and artist's smock in the classic painter's posture – a powerfully self-assertive image for a woman artist. [Picture 31]

In 1913 she showed with the Allied Artists Association and the New English Art Club, and to supplement her income she also applied to the Omega. 'One day someone said you might get a job to paint furniture and do decorative work at the Omega Workshops,' she recalled. 'Feeling brave I went to Fitzroy Square and asked to see Mr Fry. He was a charming man with grey hair and said I should come round the next day and start work. I went round and was shown what to do. Batiks. I was paid by the hour . . . and felt like a millionaire.'

Nina had a singular and spontaneous temperament, given to bold pronouncements. When, early in 1914, her work was hung with the Friday

Nina Hamnett and
Winifred Gill, modelling
Omega fashions, around
1914, standing on an
Omega rug in front of an
Omega screen. The
curtain fabric back left
looks similar to one in
picture no. 39 (page 70)
and may be Vanessa Bell's
printed linen entitled
'White'.

Nina Hamnett,
Self Portrait, 1912.

Club at the Alpine Gallery, Lytton Strachey, visiting the show, was seized with a strong desire to stroke Nina's lustrous dark hair. 'I knew that if I did, she'd strike me in the face,' he recalled ruefully, adding: 'but that, on reflection, only sharpened the desire.'

In Paris she met Modigliani, Zadkine and other artists. On the outbreak of war she returned to London, bringing a Norwegian lover named Edgar de Bergen. Both worked for Omega and when in February 1916 the firm secured a commission from a wealthy art dealer to decorate a room in his Mayfair home, they assisted Roger, together with Nina's friend Dolores Courtney, each painting a wall with a London street scene. A surviving photograph shows a remarkably integrated scheme, harmonious in colour and chaste in line, foreshadowing the poster art of the 1920s.

Nina had a slim, boyish figure and an attractive face, much given to laughter. She was physically uninhibited, like many artists, and had been on friendly terms with both Mark Gertler and the sculptor Henri Gaudier-Brzeska, then living in London, for whom she posed nude, for marble and bronze figures. 'Now is your turn,' then said Gaudier, obligingly stripping off so that Nina could sketch him.

Working alongside Nina, Roger admired her 'satyr-like oddity and grace'. They began a relationship, reflected in their paintings, which was both sexual and artistic. Both, for a while, produced still lifes – an entire Omega show in 1916 was devoted to this genre – and shared items in their works indicate that they worked together from the same props, probably in Roger's studio. This mutual contact was good for Nina: under Roger's influence she did much of her best work, including her portrait of Dolores shown at the Friday Club, using his subdued palette and firm modelling.

Roger's portraits of Nina give a good impression of her physical grace and appealing, unconventional personality. In one she is shown wearing trousers and a fisherman's jersey, holding a guitar. In another she is girlishly simple in a checked dress designed by Vanessa for Omega and probably made by Nina herself. In a third she wears a high-necked sweater, sleeves rolled up, and looks self-possessed and independent. There are also several

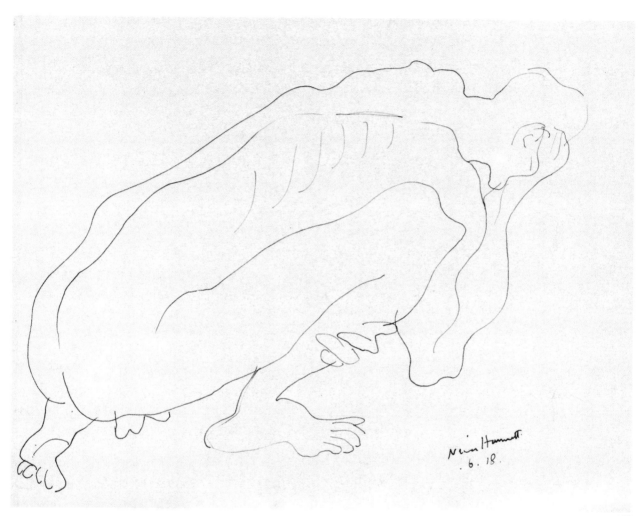

32

Nina Hamnett, *Nude Study of Roger Fry*, 1918.

nude studies of Nina, on an Omega rug – and one nude sketch by Nina of Roger crouching, which displays her draughtsmanship. [Picture 32]

But Nina did not last. She preferred roistering in Paris to serious painting in London, and although she had eleven works in the New Movement exhibition organised by Roger in the autumn of 1917, together with other pictures in the Omega show, the New English and the London Group, the end of their affair came early in 1918. 'I was rather upset when I got back to find that Nina had picked up a young man of eighteen, a drunken sodomite of pleasant manner and weak character with whom she was actually living,' Roger confessed to Vanessa. 'She's incredibly light and easily turned and acts without any reflection. . . . It's all very awkward as I have to work in the studio next door.' And he also confessed to 'a good deal of physical jealousy'.

True to Bloomsbury tenets, Roger made no attempt to retain Nina, recognizing her limitations. She was a natural whore, he concluded, albeit a very nice one, and one ought not to mind, but accept it as 'a type of character'. The truth is, however, that Nina was not really interested in sex – men seemed to like it, she commented later, 'so I let them get on with it'. For a while, Roger remained enthralled: she was 'the most fascinating, exciting, tantalising, capricious, impulsive, beautiful, exasperating creature in the world', he wrote. With her talent and his support she could make great strides as an artist; her current work was already attracting commendation. Sadly, for whatever reason, Nina wasted this opportunity.

Having barely established itself before the outbreak of war in 1914, the Omega Workshops managed to stay in business throughout hostilities, despite shortages of materials, manpower and customers, only to find itself by 1919 deeply in debt and having lost the collective energy and optimism with which it had begun. Faced with the prospect of devoting his whole time and income to rescuing it, Roger preferred to shut down – a wise if painful decision. One last endeavour was a book of *Original Woodcuts by Various Artists* (Fry, Grant, Bell, Mark Gertler, Simon Bussy, Edward Wolfe

33

Vanessa Bell, *The Tub*, from *Original Woodcuts by Various
Artists*, published by Omega Workshops in 1919. For
the earlier painting of this subject, see page 79 (no. 47).

and Edward McKnight Kauffer) published early in 1919. [Picture 33] In July came the final close-down and clearance sale.

One regular Omega client, who also became an honorary member of Bloomsbury and came into her own during the war years was Lady Ottoline Morrell. A statuesque, eccentric aristocrat, she reminded Leonard Woolf of a peacock, with her long neck, flaming hair and flowing, exotic garments. Once, she brought her daughter Julian to the Omega to choose dress fabric, selecting blue despite Julian's desire for green. Another time, Ottoline marched upstairs, followed by Winifred talking loudly to alert Nina. 'Oh God, not that old bitch,' said Nina, diving behind a curtain.

But however much they might laugh at her, as the more discerning members of Bloomsbury knew, Ottoline was good-hearted and essentially simple, with a genuine reverence for art, unlike most members of her class, the landowning aristocracy. Half-sister to the Duke of Portland, she was married to the Liberal MP Philip Morrell of the Oxfordshire brewing family, and first began inviting members of Bloomsbury to her soirées at 44 Bedford Square in the pre-war years, where despite themselves they were impressed by her eclectic guest list and elegant drawing room with dove-grey walls, yellow taffeta curtains and banks of flowers. Virginia, Lytton, Desmond and Duncan took to her at once, their enthusiasm masked by satire; Vanessa was always more reserved, and wary of Lady O's lionizing and liking for confidences.

Ottoline was tall and striking, with serpentine locks, an aquiline profile and a truly arresting appearance. Many thought she possessed a strange beauty, which is visible in photographs [Picture 34] but curiously less so in portraits; one painted by Duncan in 1913 originally incorporated a wooden chin and a necklace of real beads, in allusion to the famous pearls – reputed to have belonged to Marie Antoinette – that Ottoline habitually wore. Henry Lamb's portrait drawing is perhaps more true to life. [Picture 35]

Ottoline felt she had the soul of an artist, if not the gifts. Bloomsbury saw her as a patron, and Roger had quickly enlisted her support for the Contemporary Art Society, which bought works from living artists, as well as for the first Post-Impressionist show. Meeting up with Ottoline in Paris in October 1910, both he and Desmond were forcibly struck, not only by her outrageous hat, resembling a crimson teacosy trimmed with tiny hedgehogs, but also by her support for the new art. 'I can't tell you how it helped me to have you at such a difficult time, to help and advise,' wrote Roger after the exhibition was assailed by critics. 'I don't think I could have done it without you.'

Ottoline had 'the head of a Medusa', commented Virginia, with some awe. 'I really felt as if I'd suddenly got into the sea, & heard the mermaids fluting on their rocks.' To Lytton she was 'magnificent, splendid, sublime!' – though his exaggeration was also mocking. Towards the end of 1910 both he and Ottoline were infatuated with the painter Henry Lamb, in a curious triangulation partly played out at the Morrells' country home, Peppard. If only she were a man, Ottoline told Lytton: 'then we should get on so wonderfully'. But, as Strachey's biographer observes, since Ottoline, with her height and imperious manner, was the more masculine of the two, they did get on well, for Lady Ottoline belonged to that breed of women – like Florence Nightingale, Queen Victoria and Queen Elizabeth – that 'lit up Lytton's androgynous imagination'. Immersed in French culture for the writing of his *Landmarks in French Literature*, Lytton cast Ottoline and himself as characters in an eighteenth-century comedy of manners: he was M. le Comte, as in *Les Liaisons Dangereuses*, and she was his *chère Marquise*.

To Ottoline, Lytton was at first an oddity: his voice so small and faint, 'but with definite accentuation and stresses of tone', his legs 'so immensely long that they seemed endless' and his hands equally long, like an insect's antennae. But soon he became a dear friend and intimate correspondent, whose fantasies she enjoyed. 'At night Lytton would become gay and we would laugh and giggle and be foolish,' she recalled; 'sometimes he would put on a pair of my smart high-heeled shoes, which made him look like an Aubrey Beardsley drawing, very wicked.' Comic cross-dressing was a Bloomsbury pastime. 'Very exceeding secret,' wrote Lytton to Ottoline in

RIGHT
Henry Lamb,
Ottoline Morrell, 1912.
Aristocrat and patron,
Lady Ottoline was a
famous hostess in Bedford
Square, Bloomsbury, and
at Garsington Manor,
Oxfordshire. Wife of
Liberal MP Philip Morrell,
she had a long love affair
with Bertrand Russell.

September 1912. 'I shall be . . . in earrings! Yes! HUSH! Oh, I like them very much. . . . But of course civilised society – imagine its comments!'

Briefly, Roger Fry was equally captivated, urging Ottoline to join the Bloomsbury trip to Turkey in spring 1911, and even enjoying a sexual relationship with her one evening at Bedford Square. 'I only know how beautiful it was of you, how splendid,' he wrote immediately afterwards. 'It's made me feel absolutely humble before you.' In fact Ottoline was at this moment concluding her affair with Henry Lamb and starting one with Bertrand Russell; what provoked her dalliance with Roger is unknown, unless it be his importunity. Two months later, after his return from Turkey, Virginia innocently told Ottoline that Roger was now in love with Vanessa. He then upbraided Ottoline with gossiping to Lamb, and thence to Lytton, about his earlier advances, and she in turn feared he had talked of her relationship with Bertie, as all Bloomsbury seemed to know of it.

As her biographer Miranda Seymour remarks, it all had the atmosphere of a French farce, but the anger between Roger and Ottoline was real. Five years later, taking tea with both friends after visiting an exhibition, Virginia noted the strain between them, with Ottoline 'languid and taking refuge in her great-lady-hood, which is always depressing. They seemed to have their quarrel before their eyes.' Nevertheless, Ottoline did not boycott the Omega; indeed, in their shared liking for bold, unusual, often improvised clothes and colour schemes, Ottoline and Omega may have had a mutual effect on each other.

She favoured Turkish trousers, silk wraps and great scarves. A fervent admirer and supporter of Nijinsky, she hosted a grand party for him at Bedford Square in summer 1912 and when visiting Vanessa in 1916 she was attired as if designed by Bakst for a Russian ballet on a Circassian folklore theme, according to David Garnett: red boots below a pale blue silk skirt and short white caftan with embroidered pockets. Garnett – then usually known by his nickname 'Bunny' – had first met Ottoline at Gordon Square early in 1915 when Racine's *Berenice* was performed with giant puppets made by Duncan, and when Ottoline had resumed her soirées for those opposed to war. As Ottoline recalled of these evenings – largely occupied with impromptu dancing to different music turned out by Philip Morrell on the pianola – 'Duncan Grant was almost fierce, but full of humour and grace, as he bounded about like a Russian ballet dancer, or wound in and out with Vanessa Bell or Bunny Garnett, who looked really fierce and barbaric in bright oranges and red, a gay-coloured silk handkerchief on his head.' Lytton followed, stepping out exquisitely to Mozart with his brother James and sister Marjorie, 'his thin long legs and arms gracefully keeping time'.

Ottoline's relations with women were less satisfactory. Apart from Dorothy Brett, who adored Ottoline with an innocent passion, most women seem to have mistrusted her temperament and motives, perhaps seeing something factitious in her flattery of artists and writers. Vanessa refused to be enchanted, and at one supper party earned Ottoline's dislike by turning to Prime Minister Asquith as if in ignorance of his identity and asking politely if he were interested in politics. Some little while later, however, she was invited to tea, which included 'a most touching scene', as she reported to Roger, when Ottoline embraced her warmly, saying how nice it was to be friends again. 'Then she kissed me passionately on the lips! And so we made friends and sat and had a long talk about things.'

Ottoline herself, who seems seldom to have been malicious or even mocking, described Vanessa as being 'as beautiful as a Watts painting or a William Morris drawing' (whatever that may signify: Morris was a fine designer but neither a portraitist nor a good draughtsman) with a temperament 'like a broad river' that carried along those who chose to float with her; nevertheless 'the sea towards which she flows is her painting, above all the thing that is of importance to her'.

In 1915 the Morrells took possession of Garsington Manor in Oxfordshire, an ancient stone-built house that has come to be closely associated with Bloomsbury owing to the houseparties held there. On hearing its remodelling was complete, Lytton wrote: 'I imagine wonder – ponds, statues, yew hedges, gold paint'. According to Ottoline's biographer, the garden was Garsington's chief glory:

Lytton Strachey and Virginia Woolf
at Garsington Manor.

From the east side of the house, a stone terrace completed in 1926 led down to the main lawn. Beyond it, two pineapple-capped pillars showed the way into a large enclosed flower garden of twenty-four square box-edged beds separated by narrow grass paths and flanked by slender pointed yews like witches' hats. The beds were filled with brilliant colour, with phlox and montbretia, zinnias, marigolds, sunflowers, red-hot-pokers and snap-dragons ... At the far end of the flower-garden, under a wall smothered with climbing roses, a herbaceous border was filled with day lilies, oriental poppies, foxgloves and roses...

Beyond this lay a tennis lawn surrounded by lavender and yellow roses. On the other side of the house was a dovecot and a shady avenue leading to an ornamental pond, close-clipped yew walls and statuary. [Picture 36] On the terraces peacocks strutted and screamed.

Looking back, Ottoline remembered the scene with painful nostalgia, confessing herself 'too sensitive to ask any of those who came, "Do you remember sitting in the loggia, or standing on the stone terrace and looking down on the garden and the great spreading ilex tree? The peacocks flying there to roost, their long tails hanging behind and the grey statues against the dark yew hedges and the pond where white bodies lunged, swam, and feathery poplars and elms beyond. Did you feel as I often did, this is too beautiful, it cannot last?"'

Partly because it did not last – the Morrells sold Garsington in 1928 – and partly because it was a refuge of some splendour if not opulence during a wartime of curtailed pleasures and mounting horror, the Manor acquired a quasi-mythical status to which it seldom aspired and which seems to have been wishfully foisted upon it by others. Frieda and D. H. Lawrence were early visitors, Lawrence initially hoping that Ottoline would make it the nucleus of an ideal community where the 'new life' would be born and later likening it to the fairytale place in Boccaccio where 'they all sat round and told each other the tales of the *Decameron*'.

Inside, the main rooms had Elizabethan panelling painted in dove grey, sea green and Chinese red, outlined in gilt; they were hung with brilliantly

37

LEFT
Vanessa Bell,
Still Life, 1916.
Large earthenware bowls
brought home from
southern Europe inspired
several Omega designs.

38

LEFT
Vanessa Bell,
Self Portrait at the Easel,
1912.
The printed textile in the
foreground, manufactured
in Britain for export
to Africa, was also sold at
the Omega Workshops.

RIGHT
Vanessa Bell,
Textile Designs for Omega Workshops, 1913.
Abstract designs suitable for printed linens, sold at the Omega shop in various colourways.

39

40

41

Vanessa Bell,
Bathers screen, 1913.
Produced for the Omega
Workshops, this screen
was inspired by a camping
holiday in Norfolk. 'We
had four tents and a fire
place in a ragged field
. . .,' Noel Olivier wrote to
Rupert Brooke. 'I liked to
see Duncan and Vanessa
at their pictures out in the
field.'

42

43

LEFT
Omega sitting room, Ideal Home Exhibition, 1913.
Visible are chairs, table, plant pot, lampshades, rugs,
armchair cover and curtain fabrics, all to Omega designs,
in front of a wall panel painted with a frieze of acrobatic
figures inspired by modern dance.

ABOVE
Vanessa Bell,
Design for Omega Bed-End,
1917.
This vase of flowers was
one of Vanessa's favourite
motifs, seen also in
The Tub (nos. 33 and 47).

Vanessa Bell, *Self Portrait*,
around 1915.

44

Roger Fry, *Portrait of Nina Hamnett*, 1917.
Nina was 'fascinating, exciting . . . beautiful, exasperating',
wrote Roger. The cushion fabric to the right
appears to be based on the design shown in no. 39.

coloured drapery and scattered with cushions, Omega rugs and jars of pot-pourri amid elegant eighteenth-century furniture, contemporary paintings and Philip's beloved pianola. Desmond said it was like a wonderful lacquered box, all scarlet and gold, the guests life-sized dolls in gorgeous costumes. Clive called it a 'fluttering parrot house of greens, reds and yellows'. To Vanessa, who with Lytton and Duncan was among the earliest visitors in July 1915, it was simply an accumulation of objects put together with enormous energy and 'definite, rather bad, taste'. But, she admitted, Lytton thought Garsington a creation, almost akin to that of a work of art.

Clive's remark was uncharacteristically ungentlemanly, for he was among those who benefited from the Morrells' political principles and generosity when he and other conscientious draft dodgers went to live there, pretending to work on Philip's pig farm as a way of evading military service. And it is disorienting to read of Siegfried Sassoon's visits to Garsington in 1916, while recovering from wounds and shellshock after winning the Military Cross for conspicuous bravery and before returning to the Front. For by and large the members of Bloomsbury ignored the war, or regarded it as an intrusion in their lives. Virginia, it is true, was sick or even insane for large parts of 1914–15; as Leonard said, these were years simply lost out of their lives. Declared unfit for military service, he himself worked against war for the establishment of what eventually became the United Nations; others expressed their opposition through the Non-Conscription Fellowship. Of the women, only Molly was consciously patriotic, while Vanessa devoted her energies to looking after her family, her painting and Duncan. In 1916 she rented Wissett Lodge near Halesworth in Suffolk, in order to provide a home for Duncan and Bunny, engaged in agricultural work on a nearby farm. If only there weren't a war and tribunals in the background it would be perfect, she told Lytton.

At Wissett she first set up her studio in a barn, but when that proved too cold moved to a bedroom, where she painted a picture of the pond and planned a large interior 'out of my head', as she wrote to Roger, briefly in Paris. She hoped he would be able to see work by Picasso and Matisse.

'It would be such a mercy to see some exciting new pictures again,' she added, instead of only her own works.

A little while later Duncan and Bunny were granted military exemption, on condition they continued farmwork. In the autumn of 1916 Vanessa therefore found and leased Charleston farmhouse in Sussex, where a new chapter in the Bloomsbury story began.

CHARLESTON

....

Charleston is an old farmhouse sitting snugly beneath Firle Beacon and the south Downs of the Sussex coast. Vanessa moved in, with Duncan and Bunny who had secured war-work on a neighbouring farm, in late summer 1916. The house was solid and simple, with flat walls in 'that lovely mixture of brick and flint they use about here' she told Roger, adding that the rooms were very large and many (an exaggeration) and that the Omega dinner service looked well on the dresser.

She was now fully committed to loving and living with Duncan. As her biographer writes, her tolerance, love and capacity to create freedom drew him gradually into an intimate relationship that lasted for the rest of Vanessa's life despite the fact that Duncan's sexual and sentimental passions were stirred almost exclusively by men. His affection for Vanessa was nevertheless deep, albeit undemonstrative and in the last analysis insecure. As he acknowledged, he was so afraid she would smother him with love that he feigned greater indifference than he felt, explaining in the privacy of his diary that all he could offer was slowly growing affection, on which she could depend, but no greater commitment.

As long as Bunny stayed at Charleston the situation was relatively stable. But Bunny, in turn, was both younger and bisexual, and despite Vanessa's best efforts the emotional equilibrium was unsteady. One might ask why she preferred the uncertainties of a relationship with Duncan to undivided love and conjugal commitment from Roger. Her daughter suggests that 'his very vitality exhausted her'; although full of passion, Roger's declarations had a certain exactingness that may have been difficult to live with. By

46

In the Garden at Charleston, 1921, from Vanessa Bell's
photograph album.
From left: Leonard Woolf, Quentin Bell, Julian Bell,
Maynard Keynes (standing), Clive Bell, Duncan Grant.
In the hammock, Mary Hutchinson.

contrast, Duncan's very detachment allowed Vanessa space, for her children, for her painting and for herself. Additionally, Duncan's serious but never solemn commitment to his art nourished and stimulated her own in a way Roger's did not, although she always valued his criticism highly.

She was 'nearly always very happy' with Duncan, she told Roger frankly in 1915. Despite his sexual preferences, he liked being with her sufficiently for her to be quite content. She hoped that in the future they would all be able to be 'happy and easy and affectionate with each other'. Vanessa possessed this inclusive capacity. Even when she stopped being 'in love', her daughter tells us, Vanessa needed to be loved, and in turn Clive, Roger and Duncan remained staunchly loyal, compelled partly by her need, and never losing their affection for her.

Meanwhile Clive's affair with Molly had come to an end. Early in the war they narrowly missed an air raid, making Molly suddenly realize how shaming it would be to be killed in Clive's company. As Frances Partridge has noted, Molly had one foot in the conventional world of Kensington, where such things were considered. But there are signs that the affair had lasted its natural course. 'Whether he got bored first or she disgusted I don't know,' wrote Virginia in her diary. 'Anyhow, as I could have foretold, after violent scenes lasting almost eighteen months they have parted, and he abuses her and she abuses herself — for ever having listened.' On the rebound, Molly finished a novel that helped assuage her feelings of inferiority, and was published in 1919. Meeting her at Charleston, Bunny Garnett compared her to a little brown bird, darting out to catch a conversational butterfly in mid air, and 'then, almost before I had time to wonder where she was, back glancing at me gently out of a bright eye'.

For his part, Clive had turned to Mary Hutchinson, elegant wife of lawyer St John (Jack) Hutchinson, in what was to prove a long-lasting love affair. Somewhat aloof, she did not immediately endear herself to the women of Bloomsbury. Virginia called Clive and Mary 'the parakeets', the image deriving from her malicious suggestion to Lytton that they combine to purchase 'a cheap and gaudy' parrot for Clive — 'trained of course to talk nothing but filth and to indulge in obscene caresses – the brighter coloured the better'. It could be called Molly or Polly, she concluded in a rare but characteristic burst of bitchiness.

Mary was in fact sensitive as well as stylish, though Vanessa found her a person of 'singularly little originative power' and her husband a bore who told tedious smutty stories. In 1915, before the removal to Suffolk, Vanessa borrowed a house rented by the Hutchinsons near Chichester and in the same year painted Mary in what seems a cruel style, portraying her wide mouth in a sulky pout and turning her almond eyes into disdainful dots. She was sorry when the picture was exhibited as a portrait in the 1917 Omega show, wishing it had been labelled merely as a head study. But there is no mistaking the likeness, nor the artist's essential lack of sympathy with her subject. Once, Virginia described Mary as 'mute as a trout'; although unkind, this is an apt simile for her image as presented both by Vanessa and by Duncan in a number of paintings. [Picture 48]

Nevertheless Vanessa did not dislike Mary, and indeed was rather pleased on Clive's behalf. In 1917 she painted Mary again, as the figure standing beside the galvanized bath in *The Tub*. [Picture 47] To pose, Mary wore a long chemise, later painted out when Vanessa decided that full nudity was more decent. As Frances Spalding remarks, the image is awkwardly and tensely composed, with an uncomfortable distance between figure and tub and a hint of melancholy in the three drooping tulips – which may more accurately reflect Vanessa's state of mind regarding her own position in the triangular household at Charleston rather than any feelings towards Mary and Clive. According to her daughter, it suggests that Vanessa was aware of having reached a crisis, and for many years the canvas lay in the attic untouched, 'as though the situation it recalled was too disturbing to be contemplated'. Mary was later photographed in front of *The Tub*, so she evidently did not take offence at being portrayed as a rather chunky nude.

Virginia, who had been nursed by the faithful Ka during her distressful spell of insanity early in the war, was now well on the way to recovery. She resumed her diary soon after Vanessa moved into Charleston. The

47

Vanessa Bell, *The Tub*, 1917. See also the woodcut on
page 61 (no. 33).

Duncan Grant, *Portrait of Mary Hutchinson*, 1915.

Woolfs picnicked with the Bells at Firle on 11 August and again on 9 September, together with the three MacCarthy children. Clive and Mary walked over to Asheham and on 12 September Virginia cycled to Charleston for the first time, noting that despite a dull stretch of road it was easy enough to do within an hour. Leonard arrived after tea and they cycled back together by Beanstalk Lane, a likely-looking short cut. The Woolfs had recently acquired a camera, and on 19 September they 'took a great many photographs' at Charleston – the first of many such Bloomsbury snapshot sessions. On another occasion Vanessa brought the children to tea at Asheham, Quentin eating till he was nearly sick. Duncan joined them for dinner, and at ten the Charleston group walked home over the Downs.

Wartime food was not plentiful: on the same day Virginia recorded that they were now allowed to buy more sugar and could therefore make jam, but that milk cost fourpence a quart. A year later the price had risen to sevenpence. At Charleston there was no electricity or running water, and one of Bunny's most useful tasks was to chop logs for the fire.

The first Christmas was very cold and fine. 'And then the trees, spare and leafless; the brown of the plough and, yesterday, downs mountainous through a mist,' noted Virginia, who went over for the day, reporting also that Bunny took to his bed at one point, quite without sympathy from Vanessa. Duncan arrived from London with a store of gossip, however, and Clive enlivened the feast with a booklet of his own poems – 'the prose fantastically foppish, the verse very pretty and light', in Virginia's opinion.

The look of the winter landscape is caught in Vanessa's much later view from her studio of Charleston under snow. [Picture 49] In 1917–18 the spartan conditions led to difficulties and illness, jealousies and general scratchiness, which nearly threatened the household. But this mood is not visible in Duncan's picture of the dining room done at this date, showing Vanessa painting and Bunny writing; on the contrary, its cool blues and browns convey an air of repose – though certainly the room temperature does not seem warm! It offers a gentle image of Vanessa at work, relaxed

....

and absorbed in her painting, while Duncan's unseen presence completes a comfortable triangle. [Picture 63]

Gradually Charleston farmhouse took on its artistic aspect. Almost as soon as she moved in Vanessa began painting over the wallpapers with a warm grey wash that is seen as the key to the interior richness, allowing other colours to retain their strength while muting any stridency, and softly absorbing and reflecting light. Then, writes Frances Spalding, Vanessa began decorating doors, fireplaces, architraves and skirting boards with marbled circles, linked discs, vases of flowers, loosely painted in the classical style, and other motifs. Both she and Duncan believed that the inherent ugliness of any object could be banished for ever by decoration, according to Bunny. This gave the random accumulation at Charleston a special quality, as the strange blend of hideous furniture over-painted with delightful works of art, produced a unique and astonishing effect. [Pictures 61, 62] As the Charleston guidebook says, sixty years of genial and haphazard improvisation lies behind the creation of what now seems a fresh, harmonious and frequently witty decorative scheme. One secret of this lay in the spontaneous addition of detail, rather than the imposition of a pre-determined plan; another in the fact that any mistake could easily be painted out or replaced with a happier element.

From the start the present dining room, with its door leading into the kitchen, was always used for meals. Duncan's painting showing Vanessa and Bunny at work here indicates, however, that the first table was that now in the kitchen. The room now known as Clive's study served firstly as a schoolroom for Julian, Quentin and their governess (lessons being sometimes held *al fresco*, in the garden, or beside the pond). Upstairs, the present library was originally a studio – the painted dog and cockerel and door panels were done by Duncan around 1917 when it appears that the walls were a strong blue, as at Wissett – while the room now known as Clive's bedroom was originally Vanessa's studio and then the boys' bedroom. The room originally shared by Duncan and Bunny – who recalled that at first they slept on the floor, in the absence of beds – remained Duncan's for the

....

Vanessa Bell,
Snow at Charleston, 1944.
Though painted nearly
twenty years later, this
view of the walled garden
and bare trees at
Charleston is reminiscent
of the first cold winter
there.

rest of his life; its fireplace and door panels, painted by Vanessa, are among the earliest decorations in the house. For ten years, from 1916, another bedroom was reserved for Maynard Keynes, which now contains the 'Morpheus' bed decorated in 1917 by Duncan for Vanessa, whose initials are entwined on the headboard (Morpheus is the classical god of sleep).

On the ground floor the garden room, with its French doors to the walled garden and window overlooking the pond, has always been the main sitting room of the house. Here in 1917 Duncan painted Vanessa on the sofa wearing a straw hat; here Lytton read aloud his chapters on Florence Nightingale, Cardinal Manning, Dr Arnold and General Gordon, while his listeners snoozed. The painted log box, with Duncan's decorative dancers and music-makers, also dates from this time. Vanessa's *Pond at Charleston* may well be her first canvas completed here. [Picture 60]

The Woolfs' main residence at this date was Hogarth House in Richmond, where early in 1917 they produced the first publication of the Hogarth Press, printed by hand on their own machine. This was *Two Stories*, one by Leonard and one by Virginia called *The Mark on the Wall*, an interior monologue with marked Post-Impressionist features:

> As for saying which are trees, and which are men and women, or whether there are such things, that one won't be in a condition to do for fifty years or so. There will be nothing but spaces of light and dark, intersected by thick stalks, and rather higher up, perhaps, rose-shaped blots of an indistinct colour – dim pinks and blues – which will, as time goes on, become more definite, become – I don't know what. . . .

The second Hogarth publication was *Prelude*, by Katherine Mansfield, the New Zealand-born writer whose life briefly interwove with that of Bloomsbury at this point, through her friendship with Virginia and her visits to Garsington. To the Woolfs, at first sight, Katherine (who had led a rather rackety life in the pre-war years but now had a steady partner in John Middleton Murry, soon to be her husband) seemed rather 'hard and cheap', indulging vulgarly (as it seemed to them) in perfume and make-up.

50

Vanessa Bell,
*Portrait of David (Bunny)
Garnett,* 1915.
Vanessa's likenesses were
seldom flattering but
often expressive.

RIGHT
Vanessa Bell,
Portrait of Her Son, Quentin,
1919.
Born in August 1910,
Quentin would have been
aged eight or nine at
the time of this painting.

51

But, in Virginia's words, she was 'so intelligent and inscrutable that she repays friendship' as well as being one of the few other writers attempting the same kind of innovative work. [Picture 54]

Leonard, who was much harder to please, liked Katherine enormously, recalling that no one made him laugh more than she did at that time. He also greatly admired her talent. Praise was heaped on *Prelude* in such a golden bowl that Katherine glowed with gratification, though her own liking of Virginia was edged with envy. 'I felt then for the first time the strange, trembling, glancing quality of her mind,' she told Ottoline in July 1917, comparing Virginia to injured innocents from Dostoevsky's fiction. Then, after visiting Asheham in August, she wrote to say how curious and thrilling it was that they should both be engaged in the quest for 'so very nearly the same thing' in literature.

In exchange for *Prelude* Virginia showed Katherine what seems to have been a first draft of *Kew Gardens*, a second experimental piece. 'Your Flower Bed is *very* good,' replied Katherine. 'There's a still, quivering, changing light over it all and a sense of those couples dissolving in the bright air which fascinates me.' A few days earlier Katherine had written to Virginia describing the garden at Garsington – 'the rose leaves drying in the sun, the pool, and long conversations between people wandering up and down in the moonlight' – and also to Ottoline, wondering how to convey its unique quality in prose:

> It might be so wonderful – do you see *how* I mean? There would be people walking the garden – several *pairs* of people – their conversations, their slow pacing – their glances as they pass one another – the pauses as the flowers 'come in' as it were – as a bright dazzle, as an exquisite haunting scent, a shape so formal and so fine, so much a 'flower of the mind' that he who looks at it really is tempted for one bewildering moment to stoop and touch and make *sure*. . . .

This would be, she continued, a kind of conversation set to flowers, musically speaking. It was an idea full of possibilities: 'I must have a fling at it as soon as I have time.'

This is so close in feeling to *Kew Gardens* that one wonders if Virginia took up the challenge. She had not yet visited Garsington, and her conversations are those of unknown, ordinary figures, wandering in a public park, indirectly reflecting a common wartime preoccupation with food but similarly set to the music of flowers and small garden creatures. Among the figures are two lower-middle-class women, one stout and ponderous, the other rosy-cheeked and nimble, carefully piecing together a complicated dialogue:

> 'Nell, Bert, Lot, Cess, Phil, Pa' he says I say she say I says I ses.
> 'My Bert, Sis, Bill, Grandad, the old man, sugar,
> Sugar, flour, kippers, greens,
> Sugar, sugar, sugar. . . .
> The ponderous woman looked through the pattern of falling words at the flowers standing cool, firm, and upright in the earth. . . . [She] came to a standstill opposite the oval-shaped flower bed and ceased even to pretend to listen to what the other woman was saying. She stood there letting the words fall over her, swaying the top part of her body slowly backwards and forwards, looking at the flowers. Then she suggested that they should find a seat and have their tea. . . .
> The light fell either upon the smooth grey back of a pebble, or the shell of a snail with its brown circular veins, or, falling into a raindrop, it expanded with such intensity of red, blue and yellow the thin walls of water that one expected them to burst and disappear. . . .

'Some of the conversation – she says, I says, sugar – I know too well,' commented Vanessa when she first read this story in 1918, adding that the whole text was fascinating and a great success: 'I wonder if I could do a drawing for it.' It might not have much to do with the words, she went on, but she felt inclined to depict the sugar conversation. Did Virginia remember her earlier picture of the three women talking with a flower bed in the background? That might almost be an illustration already, she added.

By November, when Virginia sent a much-appreciated parcel of cakes, soups, sausages and sardines to hungry Charleston, Vanessa was well into her woodblock designs for *Kew Gardens*, to be included in the Hogarth Press printing. These show the two women pausing by the flower bed, and also the caterpiller and butterfly whose perspective frames the rest of the text. [Pictures 52, 53] And thus, it appears, the sisters' shared commitment to their art came together once again, as the featureless faces in Vanessa's pictures were matched by Virginia's rendering of passers-by in impressionistic prose. The modernist mode of partial points of view, non-narrative tales, shifting perspectives and concentration on overall form and selected detail are dominant in both painting and fiction.

When *Kew Gardens* was published by the Hogarth Press in 1919, Katherine described its effect to Ottoline. She called Virginia a 'beautiful brilliant creature' suddenly turning into a bird and flying to a topmost bough to continue the conversation, with a bird's eye view for the insects in her story, and a bird's motion in her writing – hovering, dipping, skimming and darting, to see 'the lovely reflections in water that a bird must see'.

Talking to Vanessa and Duncan around this time, Virginia noted that they felt there was no one worth considering as a painter in England – 'no one like KM or Forster even with whom it's worth discussing one's business'. To Duncan she wrote simply that Katherine was 'the very best of women writers', adding with a smile 'always of course passing over one fine but very modest example' – to wit, herself. Though her relationship with Katherine was sometimes awkwardly jealous, both writers knew they shared a serious commitment to taking their art in new directions that was comparable to that of the Post-Impressionist painters. This led to Katherine's disappointment with Virginia's next novel, *Night and Day*, published in the autumn of 1919, which effectively belonged to the old, pre-war world, rather than that of *Kew Gardens* and the other innovative pieces Virginia was now producing.

The painters were 'very large in effect', reflected Virginia after a rainy day spent in the studio at Charleston; 'they have smooth broad spaces in their minds where I am all prickles and promontories.' Vanessa in particular possessed this amplitude, with a whole nature in use, living practically as

Vanessa Bell, woodcut illustrations to books published by the Hogarth Press.

ABOVE: Butterfly and caterpillar, from *Kew Gardens*, by Virginia Woolf.
RIGHT: Two Women.

Vanessa produced illustrations for many of Virginia's stories, and designed jackets for her novels.

well as artistically. 'A love of the actual fact is strong in her,' she wrote with admiring affection and some envy.

A few days later, when Virginia dined with Clive and Roger in London, Roger asked if she based her writing on 'texture' or 'structure'. She replied 'texture', regarding her use of phrases – not just words – as akin to the painter's brushstrokes. The talk then flowed on to Shakespeare, Giotto, Chinese poetry. It was so stimulating, she noted, to be able to say what came into one's head, and be understood. Nevertheless, she still teased the painters, writing to Duncan after one Omega show: 'Lord, how tired I got of those sturdy pots and pans, with red billiard balls attached to them.' All the same, Roger showed her how to look, pointing out small patches of black, and passages of graining 'on which the whole composition depended'. And, she conceded, 'I believe it did too.'

When Vanessa moved to Charleston, Maynard Keynes took over the lease of 46 Gordon Square, which also acted as town house for those visiting London. Clive, still officially resident at Garsington, retained a room there, and on occasion the whole tribe re-gathered, prompting Virginia to reflect on the nature of what was now commonly called 'Bloomsbury'. On 10 November 1917, for example, she noted in her diary that 'the usual people' were present, producing the 'usual sensation of being in a familiar but stimulating atmosphere, in which all the people one's in the habit of thinking of were there' – together with several mopheaded young women 'in amber and emerald, sitting on the floor'.

It was not always so harmonious – and indeed on this same occasion Leonard was 'testy, dispiriting, tepid', not enjoying the company as much as his wife. A month later there was another gathering, with Vanessa, Clive, Mary and Harry Norton. 'As usual to my liking,' wrote Virginia; 'so much alive, so full of information of the latest kind; real interest in every sort of art; and in people too . . . a sense of thoughts all liberated.' And she also observed a curious new phenomenon: the dominance exerted by Bloomsbury over the younger generation. These included those she desig-nated as 'mopheads' or 'cropheads' – girls who had bobbed their hair – such

54

Beatrice Campbell, *Katherine Mansfield* (detail),
around 1920.
Virginia Woolf was jealous of Katherine Mansfield's
writing – 'the only writing I have ever been jealous of
. . . probably we had something in common which I
shall never find in anyone else', she wrote. The artist
Beatrice Campbell was married to the poet Lord Glenavy
and mother of the humorist Patrick Campbell.

as Karin Costelloe (soon to marry Adrian Stephen) Iris Tree, Dorothy Brett and Barbara Hiles, who was enjoying the adoration of both Saxon Sydney-Turner, a Bloomsbury doyen, and Nicholas Bagenal, a young army officer of distinctly lesser intellectual pretensions.

The younger generation tramped across the Downs in brown corduroy trousers, blue shirts, grey socks and no hats on their cropped heads, said Virginia of both sexes, confessing that she could never contemplate wearing trousers herself and claiming not to be able to distinguish Barbara from Nick at a distance. With her blue eyes, curly hair and boundless energy, Barbara 'gambolled like a puppy' among the now sedater matrons of Bloomsbury, flirting with Maynard and Bunny before arousing Saxon's undying devotion. At Charleston (where she installed herself in a tent) she helped Vanessa and Duncan dye fabric and make up stage costumes, before moving on to assist the Woolfs in London with the Hogarth Press.

With Saxon she borrowed the house at Asheham while Nick was on leave from France, so that for a while their curious triangle intersected with Bloomsbury.

Barbara refused to choose, aiming to co-exist as a threesome. 'Nick and Saxon will revolve around Barbara, who twinkles rosily but modestly in the light of their admiration,' noted Virginia, who also perceived that, much as she liked him, Saxon was far less fitted for marriage. Nick offered more solid value, Saxon only a cold-blooded and essentially abstract attachment, being now too settled in his bachelor ways. And Nick's case was more urgent, he being in constant danger of death in Flanders. In January 1918 Barbara agreed to marry Nick, while still insisting 'nothing will change'. Underneath, she was fearful that he would not come up to Bloomsbury standards.

Virginia wrote a long and mockingly satirical account of the decision to Vanessa, who replied sceptically, 'How anyone with the imagination of an owl can conceive of life as she conceives of it passes me,' she declared; 'half the year with one, half with the other, a child by each, etc., and no one to have any jealousy or cause for complaint, and she like a looking glass in the middle reflecting each in turn.' But surely something of Vanessa's own disregard of convention also helped encourage Barbara's aspiration. Nick returned to the war, and in April the Woolfs went to tea with Barbara and Saxon at her studio in Hampstead. It was almost too perfect an illustration of the Post-Impressionist style of interior decoration for Virginia's taste: 'even the black and white cat seemed decorated by the Omega.' To allay Barbara's fears, Virginia promised 'kindness' towards poor Nick, lest Bloomsbury's disapproval be too keenly felt. Barbara was already pregnant with Nick's child, Judith, born in November 1918, and as Vanessa predicted, Saxon lived on, faithful and solitary, like a poor old bachelor.

Vanessa, according to her sister's exaggerated account, had been living 'like an old hen wife' at Charleston, among ducks, children and chickens. According to Roger, however, she had triumphed. 'You have done such an extraordinarily difficult thing without any fuss,' he told her, having despite all obstacles kept on good terms with the 'pernickety' Clive, retained Roger as her devoted friend and generally got all she needed for her own development as well as being a splendid mother. 'I don't think you ever need doubt yourself,' he added. 'You have genius in your life as well as your art, and both are rare things.'

Clive concurred, as Virginia recounted after the conversation on texture in painting and prose at Roger's studio in Fitzroy Street. 'Yes, she's quite sublime,' he said, in response to Roger's praise of Vanessa's personality, adding that her latest painting of apples was one that marked a new stage in her career.

Vanessa herself was less sure. Early in 1918, along with half the population of the country, she succumbed to the influenza epidemic, and she also had domestic difficulties over the education of Julian and Quentin, who were becoming unruly. Duncan, however, was growing closer, and in the spring of 1918 Vanessa conceived his child. Though this hardly marked a change in their relationship – Duncan's romantic heart continued to be stirred by young men – the large number of paintings he made of Vanessa in this period is testimony to more than mere availability; several show her during the stages of pregnancy, and therefore when carrying his child. As painters both had now turned away from abstraction, like most other British artists; among other new projects Vanessa planned a series of woodcuts with which she continued when pregnancy made painting awkward and tiring. 'Oh Lord, I shall be so glad when I no longer enclose a baby!' she told Roger wearily at the end of November.

Earlier in the year Duncan had persuaded Maynard to bid on behalf of the British government for works from Degas's collection being auctioned in Paris. Among other things, Maynard acquired for himself a small painting of apples by Cézanne, which was visually devoured both at Charleston (where on delivery it was left in the hedge, like other parcels) and at Gordon Square, where Roger was like a bee on a sunflower, intoxicated with delight, as Virginia reported to Nick Bagenal, now at home recovering from war wounds:

> Imagine snow falling outside, a wind like there is in the Tube, an atmosphere of yellow grains of dust, and us all gloating upon those apples. They really are very superb. The longer one looks the larger and heavier and greener and redder they become.

Vanessa and Roger debated the exact hue of the pigments used, and when the picture was carried into the next room it immediately showed up the existing canvases, like a real gemstone among sham ones. This solidity of shape and colour was what the Bloomsbury artists aimed for, and what they missed through the wartime years of deprivation – material, cultural and international. A comparable effect, in textured phrases, is conveyed in *Blue and Green*, Virginia's short experimental prose:

> The pointed fingers of glass hang downwards. The light slides down the glass, and drops a pool of green. All day long the ten fingers of the lustre drop green upon the marble. The feathers of parakeets – their harsh cries – sharp blades of palm trees – green, too; green needles glittering in the sun. But the hard glass drips on to the marble; the pools hover above the desert sand; the camels lurch through them; the pools settle on the marble; rushes edge them; weeds clog them; here and there a white blossom;

the frog flops over; at night the stars are set there unbroken. Evening comes, and the shadow sweeps the green over the mantelpiece; the ruffled surface of ocean. No ships come; the aimless waves sway beneath the empty sky. It's night; the needles drip blots of blue. The green's out.

Vanessa's child by Duncan was born on Christmas Day 1918 and named Angelica (at Virginia's suggestion). Though her paternity was no secret within the Bloomsbury circle, publicly she was known as Clive's child, and indeed herself grew up believing this was so, to her later confusion. This situation is curiously mirrored in Vanessa's picture of her husband (they were never divorced) with 'his family' – comprising Julian, Quentin and Angelica.

Charleston has been identified with Bloomsbury for so long that it is difficult to believe it was not always so. Something of what the place meant, especially to Vanessa, is conveyed in Duncan's painting of her in the hammock, with the children playing in the walled garden – a place where everyone could be together, but independently active. [Picture 59]

During the war Lytton had finished his new book, the biographical analysis of four *Eminent Victorians* that chimed with the iconoclastic mood and was to make his name. He went to Richmond before delivering the manuscript and Virginia, who had seen him seldom in the past few years, noted again his gentleness and sweet temper, as well as his wit, and supple, infinite intelligence – 'not to be replaced by any other combination'. As in art, his writing broke new ground.

He also spoke of his own domestic situation, which rather surprised and puzzled his friends. For he had set up house with one of the cropheads who liked to be known as Carrington and who had been a Slade student and an Omega artist alongside Barbara and Brett. Despite 'old' Bloomsbury's misgivings she proved a permanent addition to the circle and opened a new chapter as well as a new location in the history of the group, with her steadfast devotion to Lytton and odd blend of the forthright and the fickle.

As Frances Partridge has noted, Bloomsbury was never a tight, enclosed world, but a network of mutual friends engaged in their separate activities, sustained by candour, humour and genuine interest in everyone's affairs.

CARRINGTON
AND COMPLICATIONS
················

At first Carrington disliked Lytton, or perhaps camouflaged the attraction she felt with hostility. Creeping up to his bedroom with a pair of scissors, intent on cutting off his beard, she was disarmed when Lytton opened his eyes (was he really asleep?) – and in an instant realized she was in love.

'What shall we do about the physical?' asked Lytton a few days later, when she confessed her feelings. 'That doesn't matter,' replied Carrington, thereby solving her own problem of how to reconcile love with a deep distaste for sex and indeed all female aspects of her own body; how she hated the floppy bits, she wrote. Probably the happiest time of her life was a short walking holiday with Lytton at the beginning of their relationship, when she came close to what she described as 'my day-dream character', dressed as a boy. [Picture 56] 'But the probability of us both being arrested the first night – *you* for the offence that I am not a disguised female, and me for the offence that I *am!*' she wrote in gleeful anticipation. And afterwards she was grateful. 'Dearest Lytton I can never thank you enough for these weeks,' she told him. 'I did not realise how happy I had been until this evening.'

'Dearest, dearest Carrington, one cannot think of Lytton without thinking of you,' wrote Vanessa after Lytton's death. 'It is owing to you that there is nothing to regret . . . and his friends would love you for that if for nothing else.' And, although Carrington cannot be said to have achieved comparable fulfilment, it is nevertheless true that in personal and artistic terms Bloomsbury offered her both the freedom and affection she craved.

Mark Gertler,
Portrait Sketch of Carrington,
1913.

55

Carrington, thumbnail sketch of Lytton Strachey and herself, embarking on a walking holiday, 1917. 'Hours were spent in front of the glass last night strapping the locks back', she wrote, 'and trying to persuade myself that two cheeks on the top of a hoe bore some resemblance to a very well nourished youth of sixteen.' Carrington's letters were always enlivened with drawings.

a vision

56

Born in 1893, the daughter of an elderly ex-colonial father and a mother against whose suburban gentility she rebelled, Dora Carrington was a prize-winning art student in the years of the first Post-Impressionist exhibitions. At the Slade School she joined forces with other women students – Barbara Hiles, Ruth Humphries, Alix Sargant-Florence and the Hon. Dorothy Brett – a spirited group bound together by their will to become good painters, who signalled their determination by adopting the masculine habit of using surnames only. By her second term Carrington had dropped Dora, for ever. She also bobbed her hair – a revolutionary gesture in those early days, akin to abandoning one's bra in the 1960s. (It was envy as much as anything that made Virginia call them the cropheads.)

They worked alongside a talented generation of male students, who included Stanley Spencer, Paul Nash, C. R. W. Nevinson and Mark Gertler, the 'poor Jewish boy from London's East End', with whom Carrington became entwined in a difficult and long-drawn-out love affair. 'I will tell you why I want you. I find it impossible to paint without some person at the back of my mind,' wrote Mark. 'I mean that since I got to know you, I have thought of you with every stroke I do. Now I find that I want you to see all that I paint.'

As Carrington's brother Noel has observed, it is doubtful whether Mark offered as much reciprocal support as he demanded, but the shared commitment to art was important. Carrington also responded to Gertler's intense, dramatic temperament and dark cherubic looks. For his part Mark painted a bold portrait of Carrington with her bobbed hair, making no concessions to simpering femininity but well depicting her expression of determined independence and gamine humour.

Her own self-image is conveyed in a 1913 drawing of a cropheaded student in supposed fancy dress, wearing a soft peaked cap and voluminous workingmen's trousers held up with a leather belt. [Picture 1] Carrington was a striking personality at the Slade, according to Paul Nash, with her turned-in toes, startlingly blue eyes and hair in a heavy golden bell. 'I got an introduction to her and eventually won her regard by lending her my braces for a fancy-dress party. We were on the top of a bus and she wanted them then and there,' he recalled.

All her life Carrington retained girlish traits, never really wishing to grow up. According to Bunny Garnett, she lisped like a child confiding a secret; while to her brother she appeared to have a fixed determination to regard the world as a place of brightness and promise, free expression and creative action. But, as Leonard Woolf remarked later, her 'inordinately female' character was made up of a thousand contradictory impulses, one inside the other like Chinese boxes; and she remained chronically evasive and untruthful, unable to relinquish the 'complicated calendar of deceptions' that had first secured freedom of manoeuvre from family prohibitions. When she returned home after featuring in a newspaper report on the Chelsea Arts Ball her mother wept, her father sermonised, and a neighbour scolded, saying she hoped Dora didn't really know that awful man Augustus John, with three wives! Even to be briefly associated with him was enough to ruin any young woman's life. To escape such attitudes, Carrington early adopted an obstinate evasiveness.

In artistic circles, however, freedom from bourgeois conventions brought with it the pressure to engage in free sexual relations. Carrington's relationship with Mark foundered on his sexual demands, re-inforced by other friends who sought to persuade Carrington into his bed. At Garsington (or Shandygaff Hall, as she wittily re-christened it in allusion to the crackpot inhabitants of Tristram Shandy's ancestral mansion in Lawrence Sterne's novel) she was pursued by both Morrells, as she reported to Lytton:

> Then suddenly without any warning Philip after dinner asked me to walk round the pond with him and started without any preface to say how disappointed he had been to hear I was a virgin! How wrong I was in my attitude to Mark. . . . Ottoline then seized me on my return to the house and talked for one hour and a half in the asparagrass bed, on the subject, far into the dark night . . . really I do not see why it matters so much to them all. . . .

57

Carrington, left, with
Iris Tree at Ham Spray,
Wiltshire, 1929.

'Aspara*grass?*' replied Lytton. Carrington's letters often made him laugh out loud.

At Garsington she posed naked as a 'living statue', embracing a sculpted figure on the terrace, as a sort of artistic joke. It is not known who took the photograph, but after such a display one can understand why friends were puzzled by her inhibitions in other matters.

The Woolfs asked her to illustrate the first Hogarth Press book, for which she produced small but striking woodcuts. Ottoline said Lytton would end up marrying Carrington, according to Virginia. 'God!' replied Lytton. 'I'll never marry anyone.' 'But if she's in love with you?' ' Well, then she must take her chance.' 'You like me better, don't you?' Virginia persisted, remembering his hastily revoked proposal in Gordon Square.

He said he did, and they laughed together, at Carrington's expense. But later Virginia acknowledged Carrington's good qualities, and Lytton's failings. Had she herself married Lytton, she would have found him querulous, she wrote. Moreover, no Strachey had ever done anything adventurous: 'never an Omega, never a Post-Impressionist movement, nor even a country cottage. . . . Even in the matter of taking Tidmarsh Lytton had to be propelled from behind, and his way of life insofar as it is unconventional, is so by the desire and determination of Carrington.' This was perceptive. For all his incisive intellect, Lytton could be passive and indecisive in response to people and events.

The house was very old with gables and lattice windows, Carrington reported to Lytton on finding the Mill House at Tidmarsh in Berkshire, where they first set up home together. The miller assured her that servants would be easy to find, there was an apple orchard and 'electric light in every room! I'm wildly excited.'

So at Tidmarsh in 1919 Carrington and Lytton settled into a sexless relationship that otherwise looked more or less like a marriage, albeit with freedom of movement on either side. Carrington gained a partner with no rights over her actions except those of affection, while Lytton gained a devoted housekeeper and friend. Theirs was thus a close, even loving,

Carrington, *Tidmarsh Mill*, around 1918.
At the Mill House (behind trees to left) Lytton and
Carrington set up house together and he wrote
Queen Victoria (1921).

relationship, but hardly intimate or egalitarian. Lytton retained his right to fall violently but vainly in love (as was his habit) with pink-cheeked young men, who in so many respects resembled Carrington, just as he himself bore more than a passing likeness to her invalid father, with a long beard and long legs wrapped in a rug.

It was at the Mill House that Carrington painted and drew Lytton, lying in a deckchair or reading in the library or before the fire, his legs stretched out to the mantelpiece and his almost equally long fingers fastidiously turning the pages of a book. [Picture 58] She painted the Mill, too, with its red-tiled roofs reflected in the still water of the mill-leat, into which she introduced an imaginary pair of black swans whose colour both complemented the dark weatherboarding and cleverly undercut the pastoral nature of the scene. [Picture 58] For this was no sentimental idyll, but a world that depended on her boldness to create it as she desired.

She also painted a striking portrait of Lytton's mother Lady Strachey, 'looking like an Empress'. As she told Lytton:

> She is superb. It's rather stupid to tell *you* this. I am painting her against the bookcase sitting full length in a chair, in a wonderful robe which goes into great El Greco folds. . . . So the effect is a very sombre picture with a black dress and mottled cloak, and the brilliant orange down the front of her dress. She looks like the Queen of China. . . . [Picture 65]

Vanessa's portrait of Lady Strachey, painted a year or so later, conveyed a similar impression, only slightly less regal: a matriarchal image that foreshadows her own self-portraits in later life.

Unlike Vanessa, whose art lay at the centre of her being, Carrington refused to sell or to exhibit. With regrettably feminine loss of ambition, the serious pursuit of art that marked her days at the Slade gave way to that of an amateur, so that she painted only when the impulse and circumstances prevailed. She was pleased with her oil portrait of Lytton, she confided to her diary, but dreaded showing it to anyone. She wanted no agony of soul, she wrote, adding that this was not vanity, for she did not care what others

59

Duncan Grant,
The Hammock, 1923.
Clockwise from centre:
Vanessa, lying in
hammock; Angelica,
walking down path;
Quentin, gently rocking
the hammock; Sebastian
Sprott, the boys' tutor;
Julian on the pond in the
punt.

60

Vanessa Bell, *The Pond at
Charleston*, around 1917.

Charleston Farmhouse
today.

LEFT
Duncan Grant's Studio,
with painted fire surround
and screen.

BELOW
Clive Bell's study, looking
out on pond, with
painted fireplace, logbox
and tiled table. Henry
Lamb's portrait of Clive
(no. 4) hangs above the
bookcase. The main
picture, by Frederick
Etchells, seems to refer to
Clive's huntin' shootin'
fishin' background.

63

Duncan Grant, *Interior at Charleston*, 1918. An early view
of the dining room. Vanessa is, as ever, seated at her
easel, painting the bowl of fruit on the table, at which
Bunny Garnett is writing. The third figure, who
completes the triangle, is the unseen painter, Duncan.

Carrington,
Lytton Strachey, 1916–17.

64

Carrington,
Lady Strachey, 1920.
A portrait of Lytton's
mother. 'She looks like
the Queen of China',
wrote Carrington.

65

said, only the 'indecency' of displaying what she had given her heart to. The only works she relished being seen were the inn-signs she painted for pubs around Tidmarsh: the Greyhound, the Roebuck, the Spread Eagle – attractive but essentially 'minor' productions..

It is as if Carrington had unconsciously used her talent to avoid the kind of conventional marriage otherwise mapped out for her, but that having found her niche in bohemian Bloomsbury she had no more need of artistic ambition. Some biographers have blamed Lytton for Carrington's failure as a painter, but the truth is more complex. In fact, he encouraged and admired her painting, and later paid for a studio where she could work. As Frances Partridge suggests, Carrington seems to have relinquished the necessary seriousness towards art. 'It's as if she didn't stake her all in art because she'd staked it in Lytton.' And perhaps Lytton did not insist, because he knew Carrington's confidence was too fragile to bear the stress of public exhibition and reviews.

As he was dying Lytton was to whisper: 'Darling Carrington, I love her. I always wanted to marry Carrington, and I never did.' It was not wholly true, but consoling. Yet, had Carrington married Lytton, she might not have been happier or more fulfilled. For she had a wayward streak that made her always upset any emotional equilibrium. It was she rather than Lytton who introduced new figures into the landscape of their life together, disturbing its balance – almost as if she could not bear anything so conventional as a couple, but must always create a love triangle, with all the attendant tensions this entailed.

Perhaps, too, she found Lytton too unadventurous, too much of an old fogey, wrapped in rugs and wedded to his hot-water bottle. [Picture 66] She liked long walks, riding, outdoor pursuits and holidays that involved staying in primitive accommodation in Cornwall and Spain. 'I am sitting down in that little ravine you remember, just before you turn down to the sea,' she wrote to Lytton from Bude:

> Do you remember the day you sat with me in the sun? Oh – I tried to paint but the wind blew my easel down, so I've been

forced to retreat to this little valley. It's baking hot here lying on the greenery out of the wind. And more divinely beautiful with the waters babbling over the grey rocks beneath me, and above the cliffs great white balloons of clouds racing across a cerulean sky. . . .

She was with her brother Noel and his friend Ralph Partridge, who joined the Tidmarsh household in 1920. Though it was Carrington who had first been attracted to the clean-cut, uncomplicated Ralph, when he returned her feelings her affections began to cool. At the same time Lytton developed an unrequited passion for Ralph, resulting in the sort of situation so beloved by Bloomsbury, where each member of the threesome was in love with another. Ralph found the stress intolerable, and in 1921 Carrington agreed to marry him, against her better judgement, in order to keep the household intact. 'How are the stiff-necked fallen!' she joked. 'At ten o'clock at St Pancras's shrine [registry office] I shall change my beloved name of Carrington to a less noble one.' Already, she was feeling restive.

Bloomsbury re-grouped in the 1920s with an added sense of age, achievement, and lost potential. 'How distinguished we all are!' Virginia remarked to Adrian at the opening of Duncan's first solo show in Bond Street. But though Lytton was now an acclaimed biographer, Roger the leading art critic and Maynard an internationally famed economist, not all members of the original group were equally successful. It is true that, after a slower start and greater obstacles, Vanessa and Virginia were not so far behind; yet as they all approached and passed forty, it was clear that some of Bloomsbury would not attain the eminence to which all had seemed destined. And the younger generation was pressing at their heels.

For these and other reasons the Memoir Club was convened, an 'inner circle' consisting of Bloomsbury's original members, who came together irregularly to hear each other's autobiographical 'papers'. Molly, again, was instrumental, and the first meeting took place at the MacCarthys' house early in 1920. Clive's contribution was 'purely objective' according to Vir-

66

Carrington with Lytton and Ralph Partridge, Autumn 1928.

ginia, while Vanessa began in the same vein, before being overtaken by the emotional depths she had chosen to traverse, and Duncan waxed fantastical. Molly was whimsical, declaring she had always wanted to be 'the daughter of a French *marquise* by a misalliance', while Roger told a true but unsparkling tale of a coachman jailed for stealing geraniums. Absolute frankness was stipulated, though as Leonard later remarked, this was sometimes filtered through discretion and reticence.

The Memoir Club meetings thus formed a sort of cement, binding and shaping Bloomsbury's self-consciousness. As the years went by, the group changed as members died and younger ones were elected. When Vanessa, in the 1940s, planned a conversation piece on the subject, she included ten living and three deceased members; and when the group finally disbanded in the 1950s, only four of the original members were still alive – Vanessa, Duncan, Leonard and E. M. Forster. During its time the Club heard some amusing, some serious, and some brilliant essays; those that have been published testify to the quality of thought and expression stimulated by the occasion.

After the war the painters had been free to travel again, the opportunity being most enthusiastically taken up by Vanessa and Duncan. In 1920 they travelled to Italy with Maynard, coming back via Paris, where they visited Picasso's studio and dined with the Braques, the Derains, Eric Satie and Dunoyer de Segonzac, a painter with whom Vanessa struck up an instant rapport. As Segonzac grew lyrical on the simple joys of the artist's life – the sort of thing one could never say in English – Vanessa riposted in the same spirit on the miseries and horrors, too, 'of never being able to do what one always had to go on trying to do'.

In 1921, after a summer at Charleston, they spent the autumn at St Tropez, together with Roger, the children and two servants, Nellie Brittain and Grace Germany, who as nurse, housemaid, cook and housekeeper was to become one of the longest-serving Bloomsbury employees and almost a member of the group in her own right. Young and innocent, she enjoyed the adventure of life in France, learning among other things to make a memorable *boeuf en daube*. At St Tropez Vanessa painted the view through the window known as *Interior with a Table* (now in the Tate Gallery), which has been described as one of her most satisfying paintings. Yet, compared with her view of the Italian hill town painted in Tuscany in 1912 [Picture 80], the bright, simple vision of her best Post-Impressionist work had been replaced by a more painstaking, considered style – as it were the difference between an inspired snapshot and a carefully composed photograph.

Early the next year Vanessa settled her boys at school, left little Angelica with her nanny, and went to spend a few weeks working in Paris. 'I hardly know myself with no family on my hands,' she told Maynard. 'I have begun to paint again and I feel more myself in consequence.' The result was her first solo show, at the Independent Gallery, in June, where twenty-seven paintings were exhibited, together with drawings. Despite the deep serious-ness with which she regarded her art, Vanessa seems to have been genuinely indifferent to its critical reception, pleased if works sold but never anxious (as was Virginia, for instance) over reviews.

The Woolfs had left Asheham in exchange for Monk's House, a smaller house at Rodmell, some few miles further towards the coast but still within cycling distance of Charleston. [Pictures 67, 68] As yet their London base remained at Richmond, but complicated re-arrangements went on in Bloomsbury itself (speaking geographically), revolving round Gordon Square, where several houses were soon occupied by 'core' members of the group in varying permutations. As Maynard told Vanessa: 'we all want both to have and not to have husbands and wives.'

Maynard himself had a stake in and a room at Charleston, whose costs were shared by Clive, Vanessa, Duncan and himself, and where he wrote most of his damning indictment of the post-war settlement, *The Economic Consequences of the Peace*, one of the key political books of the era. He was also – startlingly for one who had always been known for his homosexual affairs – in love with Lydia Lopokova, from the Ballets Russes, whom he married in 1923, against Bloomsbury's wishes. Though entertaining and amusing (particularly in her fractured English) Lydia – or Loppy as she was

Monk's House, Rodmell, today.

RIGHT
Hallway leading through from dining room to sitting room. Reflected in the painted mirror is Vanessa's portrait of Virginia reproduced on page 36 (no. 9).

67

RIGHT
Table top (upended to be photographed) painted by Vanessa Bell and Duncan Grant for Virginia and Leonard Woolf.

68

sometimes familiarly known – was perceived as somewhat frivolous, and her entry into Bloomsbury threatened to alter the intimacy of the inner circle. Moreover, on at least one occasion she annoyed Vanessa by wandering into the studio during 'working hours' with inconsequential requests. The Keynes' marriage, however, was a great success, at a stroke altering Maynard's sexual orientation – he never looked at a boy afterwards, according to Frances Partridge – and in time their household in Gordon Square became a key Bloomsbury residence. They also, somewhat to Vanessa's dismay, took Tilton, the nearest house to Charleston – though weeks might pass each summer without reciprocal visits.

The 1920s were the dancing years, and also the era of Bloomsbury parties, as Frances has written, at which the still youthful older generation were joined by younger members – the young MacCarthys, Bells, Stracheys, and others – and where 'continuous passionate dancing' – Blues, Charleston, Black Bottom – went on until three or four in the morning, 'when everyone reeled home to bed, some alone, some with a new temporary companion, some having fallen seriously in love. . . .' [Picture 69]

The most popular setting for such parties was Duncan's studio in Fitzroy Street, a large and shadowy space reached by an iron walkway. Some parties were more formal, in that entertainments were organized, usually in the form of dramatic performances such as that of Virginia's play *Freshwater*, which satirized the Victorian story of the Stephen family – in particular their great-aunts' devotion to Lord Tennyson and G. F. Watts, the twin 'great men' of Victorian art and literature. Once, Maynard staged a revue based on a notorious sex scandal, at the end of which he and Lydia danced the can-can, billed in the programme as 'the Keynes-Keynes'.

It was after one of these parties in 1923 that Ralph Partridge fell in love with Frances Marshall, a young Cambridge graduate then working in the bookshop part-owned by Bunny Garnett, who married her sister Ray. [Picture 70] As with most things that involved Carrington, the situation was complicated because as soon as she married Ralph she had begun another affair. Far from stabilizing the Tidmarsh triangle, the marriage had unsettled

Duncan Grant, *Design for a Screen*, 1920s.
Perhaps related to one of Bloomsbury's dramatic entertainments, usually involving much cross-dressing. In the centre, the traditional figures of Pierrot and Columbine, based on Maynard and Lydia Keynes.

69

In the Garden at Charleston, 1928, from Vanessa's photo album. Back row, from left: Frances (Marshall) Partridge; Quentin Bell; Julian Bell; Duncan Grant; Clive Bell; Beatrice Mayor.

70

it. Carrington felt circumscribed, and immediately fell in love with Ralph's friend Gerald Brenan. This affair was carried on in the Lake District, where the Tidmarsh household rented a farm, and in Spain, where Brenan lived. Both locations were recorded in Carrington's painting, and the Spanish landscape in particular was a source of strong artistic stimulation – as in her idiosyncratic views of Andalusian mountains near Yegen which antici-pate the work of Georgia O'Keefe in New Mexico. [Pictures 78, 79] 'I feel my picture is going to be one of the most beautiful in the world,' she told Gerald. 'Is it partly because you blessed it with that magic one night?'

Ralph was enraged, and a 'great row' ensued, closely observed by the Woolfs, for whom Ralph was working at the Hogarth Press. (This, inciden-tally, was now publishing T. S. Eliot's early poems, but declining James Joyce's *Ulysses*, on the grounds of its length and indecency, which indeed made the book unpublishable in Britain.) Peace was restored, however – until Ralph and Frances fell in love. Both Lytton and Carrington begged them not to set up house together, Lytton threatening to leave Carrington and saying Frances would not be welcome at their new house, Ham Spray, on the Berkshire Downs.

But soon sense prevailed. 'The Treaty has to be drawn up,' Carrington told Frances, asking if it could be compatible with her happiness to allow Ralph to remain on terms of friendship with Ham Spray; otherwise the relationship between Lytton and Carrington would be wrecked. 'The bare truth from my point of view is that if Ralph leaves me completely, or to all practical purposes completely, it really means an end to this life,' she wrote. 'I can't ask *him* to go on seeing me down here, because he really feels it depends on whether *you* can bear it. If you can't, nothing can be done. If you can, you must know it would mean everything to Lytton and me.'

'Because I love R. and want to live with him, and want him to share my life instead of being a visitor into it – I can't see how I could find this incompatible with his being fond of you and seeing you every day,' replied Frances, with a maturity beyond her years. And so things were resolved, with Frances and Ralph taking an apartment in Gordon Square and spending most weekends at Ham Spray. 'Dearest Frances, you are an owl, also a noddle, also an idiot,' wrote Carrington in one of her inimitable illustrated letters, assuring her that she was always welcome.

Carrington threw her creative talents into painting, decorating and furnishing the house, which her brother Noel called her masterpiece, both its interior and its garden. 'Books, paintings, the sweep of the Downs through the windows, an ancient gibbet on high hill tops, the garden overlooked by a weeping ilex tree, roses outside and in,' recalled Iris Tree. 'And Carrington, rose-cheeked, pouring tea, laughing upwards from under her thatch of hair, licking her lips with a delicate greediness for delicious things and topics. Lytton wrapped in a shawl, purring with delicate malice . . . his hands stretched out transparent to the flames in the firelight.'

The first Ham Spray Christmas was celebrated with a house party and a play written by Lytton, performed by himself, Ralph, Carrington, Frances and two of Lytton's new young men, Roger Senhouse and Dadie (George) Rylands. All that Frances recalled of the plot was that it involved a good deal of cross-dressing – typical of Bloomsbury dramatics.

A more usual weekend was recorded in her diary in 1927, when Julia Strachey, Lytton's niece, and the sculptor Stephen Tomlin, always known as Tommy, were fellow guests, together with Carrington's friend Alix Sargant-Florence, who married Lytton's brother James. Breakfast was taken on the veranda, where Lytton, Alix and Tommy discussed Virginia's new book *To the Lighthouse*. Lytton and Alix complained that the characters were not sufficiently solid. Tommy responded that the genius lay in conveying places and people in the same way: 'describing a garden, for instance, by making you know exactly what you would feel if you were in it, with the gap over the red-hot pokers, and so on.' It was the same with people, Frances added: Virginia did not delve into her characters' motives, but showed you, for example, 'what it would be like to be in Mr Ramsay's company'.

With this novel Virginia consolidated her reputation as an innovative writer, which had begun with her short stories and grew with *Jacob's Room* in 1922, a rather elliptical account of a young man, based on Thoby. *To the*

Lighthouse re-created her parents and own childhood holidays in Cornwall (though the book is set on Skye), as observed in part by a painter named Lily Briscoe whose work at the easel frames the episodes of the story.

In one passage Lily explains her Post-Impressionist technique to the inquiring but ignorant Mr Bankes. What was that purple triangle meant to be? he asks. Mrs Ramsey reading to her son, Lily replies, adding that there was no attempt at a likeness. For what reason were they there, then? asks Mr Bankes. Lily considers her answer before replying:

> if there, in that corner, it was bright, here, in this, she felt the need of darkness. Simple, obvious, commonplace as it was, Mr Bankes was interested. Mother and child then – objects of universal veneration, and in this case the mother was famous for her beauty – might be reduced, he pondered, to a purple shadow without irreverence.'

Later Lily contemplates the difficulties of her art. 'Where to begin? – that was the question; at what point to make the first mark? One line placed on the canvas committed her to innumerable risks, to frequent and irrevocable decisions.' All that in theory seemed simple became complex in practice, just as waves were regular when seen from the clifftop, but full of troughs and foaming crests to the swimmer among them.

This reflection is in part an account of Virginia's own art. The painter's brushstrokes were the writer's phrases; the artist's areas of colour the writer's paragraphs, laid beside others. And throughout *To the Lighthouse* there runs a male refrain that dogged both Virginia and Vanessa from their youth: *women can't write, can't paint*. At one level, the novel is a refutation of both these assertions.

Vanessa was not surprisingly overwhelmed by the autobiographical aspects. It was almost painful to have their mother so raised from the dead in the character of Mrs Ramsay, she wrote; it was 'like meeting her again with oneself grown up and on equal terms'. But she was equally impressed by the aesthetic shape and impact of the writing, which took the reader into another world, like all great works of art. She thought Lily must be rather a good painter – 'before her time, perhaps, but with great gifts?' (perhaps like Vanessa herself?) – and only quarrelled with the description of *boeuf en daube*, which surely after cooking for three days did not have to be eaten immediately it came to table, as if it had been a soufflé.

On finishing his book on Queen Victoria, Lytton had asked if he might dedicate it to 'VW' – she being utterly unlike the eponymous monarch. 'What could I like better?' replied Virginia. 'Only my inordinate vanity whispers might it not be Virginia Woolf in full? – or some unknown Vincent Woodlouse or Victoria Worms would be sure to claim the dedication.' It was a tribute to their long friendship and shared craft.

Rather in the manner of a wife, Carrington was thrilled with Lytton's success. On one occasion she told Alix that she was painting a still life of tulips, while Lytton was being wined and dined in London by Lady Cunard and other members of the 'Chelsea pseudo-aristocracy'. This habit grew with his literary celebrity, as the success of *Queen Victoria* was followed by that of *Elizabeth and Essex*. As Michael Holroyd has pointed out, Lytton had a penchant for imperious aristocratic women, in life as in his choice of biographical subjects. It reminds one of the gay predilection for operatic *divas* and musical comedy stars.

Carrington's own propensity for falling in love while remaining loyal to Lytton may have stemmed from the fact that, like so many members of Bloomsbury, she never outgrew that youthful phase that prefers the promise of romance to the responsibilities of maturity. Or perhaps again – like Lytton, Clive, Duncan, and others – she could not resist the temptations of a new love, free of all previous complications and inevitable betrayals. Leonard Woolf, succinct but unsympathetic, described her as a 'classic female': if the man pursued, she fled; if he fled, she pursued. But it was surely more complex, as she was unconsciously drawn to repeat the emotional pattern of her childhood, with invalid Lytton standing for her loved but distant father and the succession of younger men – Ralph, Gerald, Beakus Penrose – taking the place of her brothers, especially beloved Teddy, killed in the war.

Carrington,
Nude Study of Henrietta
Bingham.

But she also liked women. She became close friends with the fastidious and obscurely discontented Julia, and fell temporarily for Henrietta Bingham, who, she wrote, had the face of a Giotto madonna, and the voice of a blues singer, and made such wonderful cocktails that Carrington 'almost made love to her in public'. Originally from Kentucky, Henrietta had a perfect oval face, neat dark hair and long lashes over amazingly blue eyes. 'I dream of her six times a week, dreams that even my intelligence is appalled by,' Carrington told Alix. 'And I write letters, and tear them up continually.' She drew a nude study of Henrietta and discovered sexual, if not emotional compatibility. [Picture 71] 'Really I had more ecstasy with her and no shame afterwards,' she told Gerald. 'Probably if one was completely Sapphic it would be much easier.'

On another visit to London she was present at the screening of what sounds a most peculiar film, showing a Caesarean section, organized by the writer Raymond Mortimer, one of the younger recruits to Bloomsbury. 'Duncan and I took a seat at the far end near an Exit,' Vanessa related. The audience consisted of the whole of Bloomsbury and most of Chelsea: 'everyone you ever met or heard of – Morgan Forster, Ottoline and Philip Morrell, the Wolves, Clive, Mary, Benita [Clive's current flame], Raymond, Frances, Ralph and Carrington. There was a queue of ladies needing medical attention afterwards. Why we were all asked is a mystery! But it was certainly a most original form of entertainment.'

Too often, however, Carrington was alone in the country. As Frances Partridge recalled, she was slow to reach social maturity and did not at all wish to mix in the world of high society, always preferring domestic and country life, and always full of energy – riding her beloved pony, rearing ducks and hens, keeping house for Lytton and entertaining his friends from Bloomsbury and Oxford (the aristocrats were not invited to Ham Spray).

'Now I must run to the telephone and ring up the doctor in London and ask for a tonic for Master and order some chops and feed the horse and – you know the hundred and one little things there are for a busy housewife to do after breakfast on Wednesday morning,' she wrote with humour and perhaps a grain of bleakness; there are signs that her world was dwindling. But she laid no blame at anyone's door, believing, along with most of Bloomsbury, in the power of individual self-will. 'I still don't agree that poverty and a room of one's own is the explanation why women don't write poetry,' she wrote after reading Virginia's feminist essay *A Room of One's Own* in 1928. 'If the Brontës could write in their Rectory, with cooking and housework, why not other clergymen's daughters?' she inquired pertinently.

Conflicting emotions, felt since her days at the Slade, persuaded her that love and art were mutually exclusive. 'I should like, this year, since for the first time I seem to be without any relations to complicate me, to do more painting,' she told her diary in 1930. She was only thirty-six, but it was already getting late. She was beginning to drink too much: 'when the cat's away, the mice will play', she teased Lytton, with a drawing of wine bottles being swigged. And Julia Strachey remembered the sense of disparity. 'From a distance she looked a young creature,' she wrote of Carrington in this period; 'but if one came closer . . . one saw age scored around her eyes – and something, surely, a bit worse than that – a sort of illness bodily or mental, which sat so oddly on so unspoilt a little face, with its healthy pear-blossom complexion.'

'If when I am thirty-eight, I am not an artist, and think it is no good my persevering with my painting, I might have a child,' Carrington had written in 1920. But in 1929, when she became pregnant by Beakus Penrose, she chose an abortion instead. A baby would have fatally upset the ménage at Ham Spray.

By the winter of 1931 Lytton was dying, though the doctors did not know what his disease was. 'This is only a line partly to send you my love and partly to say that if at any time I can be of any use about household or other tiresome things, please let me be,' wrote Vanessa to Carrington, offering to send Grace to Ham Spray and trusting that Lytton had 'reserves of strength'. But sitting by him one afternoon Carrington saw a change come over his face and knew he could not live, seeing in her mind's eye 'the Goya painting of a dead man with a high light on the cheek bones'.

Superstitiously, she felt that he might live if she died, and tried to kill herself with the car exhaust. Ralph rescued her, and she was present when Lytton died on 21 January 1932, in the early hours of the morning. 'I looked at his face it was pale as ivory. I went forward and kissed his eyes, and his forehead. They were cold.'

She stayed alone at Ham Spray, though both Ralph and the Woolfs visited. 'I was never in all these 16 years happy when I was without him,' she wrote of Lytton:

> He was, and this is why he was everything to me, the only person to whom I never needed to lie, because he never expected me to be anything different to what I was, and he was never curious if I did not tell him things . . . No one will ever know the utter happiness of our life together. The absurd and fantastic jokes at meals, and on our walks, and over our friends, and his marvellous descriptions of all the parties and London and his love affairs, and then all his thoughts. . . .

Of all their other friends, Virginia was the most desolated, telling Carrington that it was a comfort to write to her, since there was no one else who knew Lytton so well. But though they grieved with and for her, there was now no one who truly valued Carrington for herself, as Lytton had done, detached as he may have been from her affairs. Alone in the house, she took a borrowed shotgun, put on Lytton's yellow silk dressing gown, aimed the gun at her heart, and pulled the trigger, blasting a great hole in her side but leaving her alive. The gardener summoned the doctor and Ralph and Frances drove from London at breakneck speed. In the early afternoon Carrington died, apologizing for all the bungling and fuss.

Forty years later, when Bloomsbury had become a part of history, Carrington's reputation as an artist was rediscovered. Exhibitions of her work are held, films made and biographies written. Her tragic death tends to overshadow her life and cast a melancholy light on earlier years. Best, perhaps, to remember her first acquaintance with Bloomsbury, and the delight with which she embraced its inhabitants. 'I have been so excited ever since I saw those artists at Charleston, and their work,' she wrote to Virginia in 1918:

Its extraordinary to be back here with my people again and the old mahogany furniture of my earliest youth. So respectable, and so highly polished. My mother's long conversations about dividends, and relations, which has gone on without a pause since I first entered the house. But I've a great deal of work to do, and there are Cotswold hills just across the lane to explore. So I expect I shall hold out for a week. And when we come back in September I'll come down, and dig the garden for Leonard like an old Mole. Virginia I did enjoy staying with you so much. . . .

In their turn, Bloomsbury enjoyed having Carrington in their midst.

Vanessa Bell,
*Grace in the Kitchen at
Charleston*, 1943.

72

IN THE SUN

....

'The ragged red tulips were out in the fields; all the fields were little angular shelves cut out of the hill and ruled and ribbed with vines; and all red and rosy and purple here and there with the spray of some fruit tree in bud,' wrote Virginia of the landscape on the French Riviera coast in spring 1925. 'Here and there was an angular white or yellow or blue-washed house, with all its shutters closed.' Below lay a circular bay of very blue water, with orange ships, ringed about by pale-coloured houses, some with pots of greenery, some with clothes drying, or an old woman watching from the window.

In 1927 Vanessa took a ten-year lease on La Bergère, a former farmworker's cottage above Cassis [Picture 81], to which was attached a tale about a miser and a shepherdess, whose picture Vanessa painted for the chimney-breast. Even after repairs and the addition of a bathroom and studio for Vanessa, the house remained small. The upper floor was Duncan's studio, reached by an outside stairway, while the four lower rooms were allocated to kitchen, living room and bedrooms for Angelica and Grace, on whose diligence the smooth running of Vanessa's various households depended, in France, London and Sussex. Adaptable and full of zest for life, she learnt French, saying later that she'd learn Chinese if she had to, in order to talk. Over the years Vanessa painted Grace on several occasions. Perhaps the most characteristic shows her mixing pastry in the kitchen at Charleston; though much later in date, the image seems to retain Grace's youthful appearance. [Picture 72]

According to Angelica, Vanessa had an unshakeable belief that 'the French were vastly superior to the English in all departments of life'. Moreover, they treated artists with appropriate respect: in France Vanessa felt she was taken seriously as a painter, in a way that she never was at home. Whether this was owing to innate British distrust of art in general, or to a more specific prejudice against women who aspired to professional status, is hard to say; certainly women artists were still regarded as a lesser breed.

'Wouldn't you like to buy another house quite near here?' Vanessa asked Leonard from La Bergère early in 1928. There was one going cheap, in a sunny and sheltered position, with its own well. In February it was already so warm that no fire was needed until the evening, and she could work outdoors nearly every day. She suspected Leonard and Virginia thought of Cassis as a hive of activity – 'Bloomsbury by the Mediterranean' – whereas in fact the solitude was wonderfully satisfying. Naturally enough, however, Bloomsbury came to visit. This same year visitors, who had to take lodgings elsewhere, though frequently sharing meals at La Bergère on the south-facing terrace, included Clive, Julian, 'the Woolves' (as they were known within the group), and Raymond Mortimer, the new Bloomsbury camp-follower.

One of the new amenities was a motor-car – mechanically temperamental and driven in much the same style by both Duncan and Vanessa – which allowed explorations and excursions, one to the asylum at St Rémy where van Gogh spent his last days. It was a pleasant place with cloister gardens and a lovely view, Vanessa told Quentin who was now aiming for a career in art. Virginia, she added wickedly, 'hoped she'd be shut up there the next time she went cracked'.

One day Lytton and Carrington came to lunch, while touring Provence. 'I'd like to stay in the country and paint,' Carrington wrote to Gerald from Aix. 'One's head instantly becomes filled with a hundred ideas for painting . . . black widows, old men with white moustaches and portfolios, nuns herding *petites peuples* in white dresses to confirmations and the students of the University arguing with each other outside the cafés.' Either on this trip or during another in 1929 she painted two Mediterranean views showing the curiously rigged fishing boats against the steep coastline of pine trees and painted houses.

To keep Angelica company at Cassis Barbara's daughter Judith Bagenal was invited to stay. Each day Grace escorted the two girls to French lessons in the town, after which they went to the pâtisserie. In the dry countryside the smell of woodsmoke mingled with that of rosemary and resin from the pines. Best of all were beachside picnics – one year Roger hired a boat to explore the many hidden bays – and swimming in the clear blue water.

It was not exactly that Vanessa neglected her children's education. Julian and Quentin were sent to a Quaker school, from where julian proceeded to Cambridge; while shortly after her tenth birthday Angelica also went away, partly at her own request. But the establishment chosen was a school 'as little resembling one as possible' where she was allowed to ignore the lessons she disliked. For Vanessa thought all formal education was a waste of time, especially for artists, who had no need of knowledge or mental training. It was, she conceded, different for buys, who might have to earn a living in other fields; and in any case with regard to her sons' education she always consulted Clive, even if in other respects he always deferred to her.

Perhaps they conferred about Angelica's schooling, too, under the curious arrangement whereby Clive took on a paternal role, despite not being her father. But since his perspective was fundamentally 'conventional and frivolous', with a tacit assumption that girls should ideally be pretty and amusing, not serious, and Vanessa's was that art was the only worthwhile pursuit, it is not surprising that Angelica's education was somewhat haphazard. Whenever she thought of what she would be 'when grown up', it was either as an artist of some kind – actress, singer, painter – or as a wife and mother. At school she therefore avoided all 'difficult' subjects in favour of music, art, French and English. In this respect such upbringing closely mirrored that common in upper- and middle-class circles at the time, where girls were not expected to train for careers or a university education. At the same time, however, Bloomsbury's daughters were not expected to be

73

Duncan Grant, *Angelica Playing the Violin*, 1934.
The decorated edge to the mantelpiece is that in Duncan's
studio at Charleston.

Duncan Grant, *Angelica at the Piano*, 1940.
Also painted at Charleston.

idle or merely decorative, for there was an unspoken assumption that artistic distinction was the highest aim in life and the only satisfying pursuit.

Later, Angelica criticized the 'misplaced permissiveness' of her mother's approach, feeling the demoralisation of not being put to the test'. Yet she learnt to paint and to play both the piano and violin, recalling that despite the meagre place music occupied in Bloomsbury both Duncan and Vanessa were more musical than they knew – an affinity attested to by Duncan's picture of his daughter playing the violin, and another, which is surely also drawn from Angelica, of a girl at the piano, painted at Charleston. [Pictures 73, 74]

At the deepest emotional level, Angelica has suggested, Vanessa thought that women were superior to men, who in her experience tended to be immature and self-indulgent. But her attitude was more humorous than censorious, and more personal than political in outlook. By contrast Virginia, in these interwar years, returned to a more overtly feminist position, such as had characterized her early work for the suffrage campaign. Now, of course, women had the vote, granted to those over thirty in 1918 and to all in 1928, though many social attitudes remained unchanged. More significantly for Bloomsbury, so did ideas regarding women's capacities in general.

In 1920 Desmond MacCarthy, now a leading literary journalist, formulated an aphorism to sum up his position on gender, saying: 'Men and women are really more alike than they can believe each other to be; but they ought not to behave to each other as though this were true.' He went on to endorse Arnold Bennett's declaration that women had never produced a masterpiece or major intellectual step in any field, and no amount of education or emancipation would alter this.

Virginia at once took issue with this. Desmond retorted that the occasional woman of genius in the 2,500 years since Sappho hardly disproved the claim, and that many men of genius had overcome greater disadvantages than women commonly suffered. Why, indeed, were there no great women painters, now such careers were within their reach? Painting was within women's reach, replied Virginia, no doubt thinking of her sister and perhaps also of Carrington 'if that is to say there is sufficient money after the sons have been educated to permit of paints and studios for the daughters – and no family reason requiring their presence at home. Otherwise they must make a dash for it and disregard a species of torture more exquisitely painful than any man can imagine. And this in the 20th century!'

It was not education alone that mattered, she continued; it was that women should have 'liberty of experience' and freedom to challenge men without fear, and that all activity of mind should be encouraged, so women might think, invent, imagine and create as freely as men. Statements such as those by Bennett impeded the achievement of such conditions, and perpetuated the 'half-civilised barbarism' of present gender relations, in social and political if not personal terms.

At this Desmond gallantly withdrew from the debate, though one suspects without altering his views. Much as she loved the 'tender, garrulous, confidential' Desmond, Virginia found his masculine egotism infuriating. He was so sure his view was the right one, she noted on one occasion. No woman of her acquaintance would call uninvited and stay for three hours without thinking she might be tired or busy or bored: 'and so sitting talk, grumbling and grudging . . . then eat chocolates, then read a book, and go at last, apparently self-complacent and wrapped in a kind of blubber of misty self satisfaction.'

One suspects that many other denizens of Bloomsbury, for all their 'advanced' ideas, held similar views on gender issues. Feminism, wrote Morgan Forster, left spots of contamination throughout Virginia's work, as if she were unable to see that the long suffragette struggle was over. No one in Bloomsbury could be unaware of Virginia's views on women and creativity, published in 1929 in *A Room of One's Own*, in which she expanded on her responses to Bennett. But one has the impression that only she and Leonard felt so strongly, or so urgently, in such a social and political manner. To others, creativity was more of a personal, individual matter, possessed by some people and not others, though perhaps potential in most, when not suppressed by upbringing and education.

More attractive, perhaps, were Virginia's flights of fantasy such as her novel *Orlando*, masquerading as a *jeu d'esprit*, in which she explored notions of androgyny inspired by her romance with Vita Sackville-West. This chimed with Bloomsbury's firmly held view that love and romance ignored gender: anyone might and did fall in love with anyone, regardless of sex. Thus, for instance, both Vanessa and Bunny had desired Duncan, and Lytton and Carrington had loved Ralph. Both Lytton and Molly had fancied the young Philip Ritchie, who died tragically young. It is true that many central members of Bloomsbury were unisexual, as it might be termed, rather than given to mix and match, but none seems to have regarded gender as the limiting factor in love, and all enjoyed dressing up in cross-gender clothes on any festive occasion.

This is somewhat akin to the storyline of *Orlando*, in which the protagonist begins as a dashing young man at the court of Elizabeth I, but changes into a woman at the Restoration, continuing as such through to the present and thus pointing up the history of disadvantage even within the aristocracy but also exploring the possibilities of both genders. 'Different though the sexes are, they intermix,' says Orlando. 'In every human being vacillation from one sex to the other takes place, and often it is only the clothes that keep the male or female likeness, while underneath the sex is the very opposite of what it is above.'

The inspiration for *Orlando* was Vita Sackville-West, direct heir to the great house of Knole but displaced by a male cousin; she was avowedly lesbian in her love affairs, while remaining wife to diplomat Harold Nicolson and mother to two boys. Tall and stylish, she liked wearing large hats and knee breeches. [Picture 75] Once, she ran away to France with her lover Violet Trefusis, in male disguise as if Violet's husband. Virginia too was seduced into a Sapphic romance, enchanted by Vita's boldness and unconscious assumption of privilege, but not blind to her limits. When Vita and Roger dined with the Woolfs, they struck sparks off each other, Roger

75

William Strang, *Lady in a Red Hat*, a portrait of Vita
Sackville-West, on whom Virginia Woolf based the
androgynous hero/ine of her novel *Orlando*.

displaying obstinate, uncompromising honesty, as Virginia noted, in contrast to Vita's indiscriminate habit of praising all things artistic – a style alien to Bloomsbury, much as they enjoyed lively, free-ranging conversation. Not till Clive arrived did the atmosphere lighten, as he deployed his urbanity to soothe Vita's ruffled plumage.

Vanessa turned her customary ironic eye on Vita, describing her on one occasion as 'as masterful as Mussolini' and on another as 'having simply become Orlando the wrong way round' – looking mannish and 'surely altogether much bigger'. But she was not unsympathetic, and seems to have genuinely liked Vita, in small doses. For Angelica's twelfth birthday, a great masked party was held at Duncan's studio in Fitzroy Street, to which Virginia came as Sappho – 'a most voluptuous lady casting her eyes up to heaven' – and Vita as 'a terrible caricature of herself gone to the bad', in a mask that frightened them all when left lying about afterwards. There followed a play, based on the fact that Whistler had once occupied the same studio, with Duncan as Sir Frederick Leighton P.R.A., engaged on a portrait of Ottoline, played by Angelica. Various interruptions followed, by Virginia, Roger, Julian, Vanessa, the Keyneses, Leonard's dog Pinka and others, with a concluding epilogue in which any stray members of Bloomsbury who had so far escaped were subjected to sharp mockery.

By this date, Virginia and Leonard were living at 52 Tavistock Square, having moved there from Richmond in 1924. It was two blocks or so from Gordon Square, where the Bells, Keyneses and Stephens were still located. One June evening Virginia and Vanessa sat in the central Square gardens while Angelica played ball with Pinka, gossiping about family affairs, including the ending of Clive's affair with Mary. Later, Virginia noted that Adrian at age forty-three was about to start his career in psychoanalysis. 'So we Stephens mature late. And our late flowers are rare and splendid,' she wrote. 'Think of my books, Nessa's pictures – it takes us an age to bring our faculties into play.' [Picture 76]

Her aunt was an enchanting, if demanding, companion, according to Angelica, with whom Virginia insisted on playing a fantasy game in

Vanessa Bell,
*Angelica Bell and Adrian
Stephen at Charleston*, 1936.
The younger brother of
Vanessa and Virginia,
Adrian was Angelica's
uncle. He and his wife
Karin became eminent
psychoanalysts.

which Angelica was Pixerina and she herself Witcherina. They pretended to fly between houses, over the trees and Downs between Rodmell and Charleston, all the while inventing improbable stories about other members of the family. Angelica's memories of this, as of much else in her childhood, are tinged with awkwardness; although she loved Virginia's make-believe she also sensed she was being subtly taken advantage of, for Virginia's own ends. And indeed many of the images of Angelica when young suggest something similar: that she was unwittingly acting out roles chosen by her elders.

Barbara Bagenal, however, recalled how much Virginia loved children, and how she enjoyed their company and games. Once, when Vanessa was planning a party for Angelica at which Roger played the White Knight from *Alice Through the Looking-Glass*, she asked the children whom they would most like to invite. As one they replied 'Virginia!', a judgement endorsed by Barbara's daughter Judith, another guest at Angelica's very special parties. Her nephews Quentin and Julian agreed.

To see Vanessa in later life, brush in hand, was to see her happy, remembered Angelica. Her working days – which meant most days – began with a frugal breakfast, after which she ordered the meals for the day. At Charleston between the wars the food was abundant and good: lots of butter, milk, eggs, roast joints and garden vegetables, followed by treacle tarts, apple pies and roly-poly pudding.

Then Vanessa would go to her studio, hoping to be undisturbed, though occasionally Grace would come to her with a problem. At one o'clock she came down to lunch, followed by coffee and a return to the studio. But the afternoons, according to Angelica, were more relaxed, and sometimes included gardening. Tea was also a relaxed moment, often devoted to friends and family – particularly when the Woolfs were at Rodmell. Vanessa would wander round the garden with Leonard, asking his advice about planting and listening to his sagas about local government and the Labour Party. Then there was not long before dinner, and Vanessa would have a bath and change into a home-made evening dress, complete with ear-rings in

Duncan Grant, *Vanessa Bell at Charleston*.

the shape of bunches of grapes.' Grace rang an old cowbell, and all gathered punctually in the dining room. After dinner there might be music, brandy and conversation in the garden room, with the scent of tobacco flowers on the air; and after everyone had gone to bed Vanessa would write letters. It was a long day with little rest, but not therefore exhausting, thanks to the high value she placed on a basic rhythm and balance in daily life.

'Suppose you are drawing a flower. If you are capable of seeing that flower with all its subtleties of form, the ways its edges recede or are sharp against the space behind, you have to try to express your feelings about those things in line,' Vanessa explained when invited to speak at her sons' school in 1925. In the interwar years both she and Duncan retreated from experimental painting, settling on a representational style in which mood and feeling were expressed by colour and form, without abstraction or distortion. The framing of subjects became more conventional, though the handling remained expressionistic rather than literal, with no attempt at photographic realism. Once, she explained to Roger that children and household responsibilities prevented her from joining a painting expedition, but that this hardly mattered because one view was as good as another. A corner of the room, the view from the window, a vase of flowers, a bowl of fruit: all had line, form, colour and the potential for expressive represen-tation, without any need for rhetorical flourish. Sometimes her brushwork can appear perfunctory, but this is the result of knowing, so to speak, how much to leave unsaid.

In these years she designed dustjackets for the Hogarth Press, including those for all of Virginia's books, using a very loose, suggestive style with freehand lettering whose subtleties match the impressionistic nature of Virginia's writing. It is a distinctive graphic style, deriving from Omega decoration, yet very thoughtful. A whole sketchbook of ideas for *A Room of One's Own* for instance preceded the final design showing a clock on the mantelpiece – a portion of a room, to be sure, but figuring the theme in a different way: to Vanessa, the equivalent requirement for female creativity was time of one's own.

37

38

RIGHT
Vanessa Bell,
*Textile Designs for Omega
Workshops*, 1913.
Abstract designs suitable
for printed linens, sold at
the Omega shop in
various colourways.

39

40

41

RIGHT
Vanessa Bell,
Bathers screen, 1913.
Produced for the Omega
Workshops, this screen
was inspired by a camping
holiday in Norfolk. 'We
had four tents and a fire
place in a ragged field
. . .,' Noel Olivier wrote to
Rupert Brooke. 'I liked to
see Duncan and Vanessa
at their pictures out in the
field.'

42

43

LEFT
Omega sitting room, Ideal Home Exhibition, 1913.
Visible are chairs, table, plant pot, lampshades, rugs,
armchair cover and curtain fabrics, all to Omega designs,
in front of a wall panel painted with a frieze of acrobatic
figures inspired by modern dance.

ABOVE
Vanessa Bell,
Design for Omega Bed-End,
1917.
This vase of flowers was
one of Vanessa's favourite
motifs, seen also in
The Tub (nos. 33 and 47).

Vanessa Bell, *Self Portrait*,
around 1915.

44

Roger Fry, *Portrait of Nina Hamnett*, 1917.
Nina was 'fascinating, exciting . . . beautiful, exasperating',
wrote Roger. The cushion fabric to the right
appears to be based on the design shown in no. 39.

In a reciprocal manner, for Vanessa's solo show in 1930 Virginia contributed a catalogue essay, in which she tried to convey her impression of the paintings – not altogether satisfactorily, since like her sister she hesitated to overload the images with interpretation. A better account of Vanessa's work was given by Roger, in which he expounded on its 'aesthetic scrupulosity' and distinctive reticence:

> Complete frankness of statement, but with never a hint of how she arrived at her conviction. It is with her a point of honour to leave it at that, never to explain herself, never to underline a word, never to exercise persuasion. You are left with the completest statement she can contrive, to make what you can of it or nothing at all, as the case may be.

With characteristic diffidence, Vanessa herself credited Virginia and Duncan (who designed the poster) for the success of the show. Within the first few days, twelve of the twenty-seven paintings sold. Maynard Keynes bought some large (female) nudes, but the sale that best pleased the artist was to a 'stray customer' who wandered in 'and bought that little grey landscape of the farm at Fontcreuse and said he'd bring his wife to look at the tulips in a green jar'. He must, Vanessa concluded, be one of those infrequent Englishmen who really liked painting.

'I have now at least six stories welling up in me,' noted Virginia in 1925, likening her technique to that of painting:

> This dash at the paper of a phrase, and then the typing and retyping . . . the actual writing being now like the sweep of a brush; I fill it up afterwards. Now suppose I might become one of the interesting – I will not say great – but interesting novelists? Oddly, for all my vanity, I have not until now had much faith in my novels, or thought them my own expression.

Both sisters urged each other to more ambitious projects, Virginia encouraging Vanessa to work on larger canvases and Vanessa supporting Virginia's most innovative writing. In 1931 Virginia published *The Waves*, a non-representational novel originally inspired by Vanessa's account from the

Vanessa Bell, *Interior with Housemaid*, 1938. Painted at Charleston after Julian Bell's death in Spain and shortly after the conversion of this ground floor room into Vanessa's bedroom. The empty chair and open desk indicate the invisible occupant, and possibly also her precious store of letters to and from Julian. 'There is a language simply of form and colour than can be as moving as any other,' she wrote.

south of France of a large moth knocking against the window. It is constructed from the interior monologues of six friends – three men and three women – across the years, and was conceived of as 'an abstract mystical eyeless book: a playpoem' which formed itself slowly in Virginia's mind. Written in a style that is like that of a musical composition for complementary instruments, it articulates the essence of the Bloomsbury group, growing old together and apart, but held by invisible cords. The six intertwined lives are likened to the facets of a red carnation, illuminated against dark yew trees, 'built up with much pain, many strokes':

> 'Marriage, death, travel, friendship,' said Bernard; 'town and country; children and all that; a many-sided substance cut out of this dark; a many-faceted flower. Let us stop for a moment; let us behold what we have made. Let it blaze against the yew trees. One life. There. It is over. Gone out.'

The six interlaced lives, sharing and exchanging memories, surely owe much to the reminiscences of the Memoir Club, as well as to the many meals shared by the denizens of Bloomsbury.

> 'Look,' says Rhoda, as they gather in a restaurant, 'listen. Look how the light becomes richer, second by second, and bloom and ripeness lie everywhere; and our eyes, as they range round this room with all its tables, seem to push through curtains of colour, red, orange, umber and queer ambiguous tints, which yield like veils and close behind them, and one thing melts into another.'

According to Stephen Spender, a younger writer who was sometimes critical of Bloomsbury, *The Waves* was a harmony of interrelated lives and the artist's multi-faceted mask of human loneliness. Reading it left Vanessa 'rather gasping, out of breath, choking, half drowned' in emotion and admiration. And she confided that she had been working for the past two years on an 'absurd great picture' which, if she could achieve what she wanted, would have 'some sort of analogous meaning' to what her sister had done. How could she explain in words? But, to her, 'painting a floor covered with toys and keeping them all in relation to each other and the figures and the space of the floor and the light on it' meant something similar to what Virginia was striving for.

This canvas was that of *The Nursery*, a large picture now lost (possibly destroyed by bombing in World War II) depicting two children with a mother and nurse, which presents 'a nostalgic evocation of motherhood' as well as intimations of loss as children grow older. A companion piece, painted in 1932, depicts two women in what appears to be the painter's studio, complete with cast-iron stove and coal scuttle. It is tempting to read the pair as a commentary on Vanessa's life, divided between art and domesticity. A gulf separates the two figures, whose poses half-mirror each other, even while they are held in formal balance.

Another image from this period is that of Angelica and her uncle Adrian, painted at Charleston. And of course Vanessa continued to paint Duncan, and he to paint her. Indeed, looking at the pictures, one would hardly credit that Duncan's emotional entanglements with young men still brought tension and turbulence to the household. Perhaps, however, they prevented it falling into complacency and dullness.

When in London both artists now worked and more or less lived at 8 Fitzroy Street, the studio reached by means of a covered iron walkway through to the mews behind. Here Duncan had a small bedroom and a large painting room and Vanessa a similar amount of space containing a larder, kitchen (with bath), dining area, bed and painting area partly closed off by a curtain. Flossie, the housekeeper from Gordon Square, came over each day to clean, shop and cook lunch; thereafter Vanessa had a 'greater sense of freedom' in her daughter's words. 'Tea would be reduced to a cup of liquid and a delicious cigarette,' often shared with Virginia over the studio stove. In the evenings friends might come to supper, or they would go to the theatre, cinema or ballet with Angelica, who had her own bedsitting room at the top of the Gordon Square house.

Angelica herself first became aware of 'Bloomsbury' as a cultural entity in her teens, partly through reading Virginia's books, though naturally she took most of it for granted. It was, she recalled, a matter more of people than places – or including places that a number of people had made their own, such as Gordon Square, Fitzroy Street, Charleston and Monk's House. Gordon Square was 'intensely Bloomsbury' owing to the several families living there, and after an absence she would return to Bloomsbury as to a village, with a distinct feeling of coming home. Fitzroy Street, however, was clearly painter's rather than writer's territory; as such it made the hair on writers' necks bristle a little with the emphasis on the visual dimension that they did not fully understand even while finding themselves refreshed and stimulated. But the painters also penetrated writers' territory, with the interior decorations done by Vanessa and Duncan for all members of the group, visible in the background of the portraits of Leonard and Virginia taken by photographer Gisele Freund in 1939. 'In Tavistock Square the painted walls impressed me like a salute from one sister to another,' Angelica has written. 'They were like a flag with the word *Bloomsbury* clearly marked on it, and yet how different the atmosphere of each place.' Vanessa's studio was a workshop where things were constantly being made and altered, whereas Virginia's rooms were an elegant, if not fashionable, background for her distinctive and remarkable personality. [Picture 86]

Decorative art in the Omega tradition still flourished, in the painted walls and in commercial commissions for textile designs and ceramics. One of these was a dinner service for the Kenneth Clarks, decorated by Vanessa and Duncan with portraits of illustrious women: twelve queens, twelve writers, twelve 'beauties' (including 'Miss 1933'). That should please the feminists, declared Vanessa, with more optimism than accuracy. [Picture 87]

At Tavistock Square Virginia and Leonard lived on the upper floors, above a solicitor's office, while the Hogarth Press was located in the basement, together with a garden room in which Virginia wrote. It was, recalled John Lehmann, (appointed the Press's business manager in 1930), a large square workroom with a skylight, also used as a stockroom and there 'in the midst of an ever-encroaching forest of books was her desk, stuffed and littered with papers, letters and innumerable half-finished manuscripts', where Virginia would stay for hours, writing steadily at novels, stories,

Vanessa Bell,
Portrait of Leonard Woolf,
1940.

reviews, or her own diary. Lehmann, whose admiration for her fictional sensibility and awareness of the paramount importance of technique and experiment was boundless, felt that she was not happy unless she was writing, 'her pen moving over the paper in that thin, elegant, intellectual handwriting with the beautiful flourishes'. She was, however, also an enchanting conversationalist, full of curiosity over others' lives and bubbling with impractical ideas that Leonard had to pull firmly to the ground.

86

Gisele Freund, portrait
photograph of Virginia
Woolf, at 52 Tavistock
Square, 1939. Wall
decoration by Vanessa
Bell. The house was
destroyed by bombing
in 1940.

There were visitors, too: Roger 'eagerly spinning his latest art theories', or Aldous Huxley leaning against the mantelpiece as he discoursed, or Julia Strachey and the melancholy, neurotic Stephen Tomlin, who in 1931 finally persuaded Virginia to sit to him for his celebrated portrait bust.

Frances Partridge recalled Virginia's taste for the fantastical, remembering that when sometimes she went to Charleston for the weekend and the Woolfs came over for a meal, Clive would gently coax Virginia into one of her dazzling impromptu performances: 'wild generalisations based on the flimsiest premises and embroidered with elaborate fantasy' that were sent up like rockets and greeted with laughter and cunningly placed interjections by Clive and Duncan. Once at Rodmell, however, Virginia deliberately needled Frances, mocking her university education in a way that betrayed envy but was painful to the younger woman. Then, just as capriciously, Virginia repented, turning on the full force of her kindness and sympathy and utterly captivating her erstwhile victim.

Her niece Ann Stephen had comparable memories, recalling both a fantastical visit to the theatre with the Woolfs and an occasion when Virginia visited Ann at college, and met some of the students for coffee and conversation. 'It was not that anything new or startling was said,' wrote Ann; but Virginia's natural interest in what the young women were doing and thinking brought out the best in all.

Angelica's memories of warm weekends in Sussex are evocative of these interwar years. At Charleston, she recalled, tea was brought into the garden on a low table, while Clive and Virginia teased each other from canvas chairs that squeaked when they moved. Clive pulled on his pipe; Virginia often wore a hat. At Monk's House they had tea indoors, in the 'dimly green' dining room below the level of the garden, where Virginia was egged on to more hilarious fantasies, waving her cigarette with infectious excitement, until Leonard quelled her with a sardonic comment.

Such memories are many. Bloomsbury might be in its maturity, but it still gave out a golden glow.

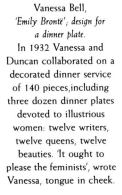

Vanessa Bell,
*'Emily Brontë'; design for
a dinner plate.*
In 1932 Vanessa and Duncan collaborated on a decorated dinner service of 140 pieces, including three dozen dinner plates devoted to illustrious women: twelve writers, twelve queens, twelve beauties. 'It ought to please the feminists', wrote Vanessa, tongue in cheek.

DARKENED DAYS

·················

If Lytton's death in 1931 was the first major break in Bloomsbury's ranks, a greater blow was that of Roger in 1934. Some few months earlier Vanessa's portrait of him had been on show at her latest solo exhibition, and she had written teasingly to draw him back from a trip to Sicily, saying she needed him more than ever for the sake of constructive criticism. But then, in the autumn, he had a fall at home and died soon afterwards in hospital. Vanessa was in Sussex when the news came and the next day Angelica heard her mother howling in sorrow behind her closed bedroom door; Roger was the friend she and Bloomsbury could least bear to lose. Though a latecomer to the group, his ideas and presence did much to shape its identity. He was 'the most magnificent, the most loveable of all our friends. He will never die because he is the best part of our lives,' wrote Virginia to Roger's lover and companion for the past five years, Helen Anrep. A year later Virginia agreed to write his biography, a labour of love but some trouble, for many irregular aspects of Bloomsbury life had necessarily to be concealed from the wider world.

In 1937, at the age of nineteen, Julian Bell volunteered as an ambulance driver for the Republican side in the Spanish Civil War. Within six weeks he died of shrapnel wounds, a fearful loss to Vanessa, who had loved him with a special intensity. 'I thought when Roger died I was unhappy,' she told Virginia. Now, 'I shall be cheerful, but I shall never be happy again.' Suddenly, both sisters felt that the malign fate that had stalked their early years, with the untimely deaths of their mother, sister Stella and brother Thoby, was again pouncing upon them.

Soon after Julian's death Vanessa told Angelica that Duncan was her father. But nothing more was said, and Duncan himself never acknowledged the fact, so that to Angelica he remained adored and delightful, but never paternal. 'There were no fights or struggles, no displays of authority and no moments of increased love and affection. All was gentle, equable, and superficial,' she wrote later.

But there was a grave, if indirect struggle when Bunny Garnett began an affair with Angelica. She had remained ignorant of the past history of his sexual involvement with her parents during World War I – as also of Bunny's declaration that he would one day marry Angelica. In the years since her birth, Bunny had been married to Ray Marshall, who was now dying of cancer. As it seems, from some desperate need to ally himself with youth and health, he pursued Angelica relentlessly. She felt unable to resist. Vanessa hovered anxiously, trying to dissuade Bunny and to calm Duncan, who was upset and jealous, aware of the cruel streak in Bunny's nature. Had the situation been less fraught with unavowed emotion, Angelica has written, she might have been able to enjoy an affair without fuller commitment; as it was, the turbulent, unspoken feelings it provoked were incomprehensible and menacing.

In April 1938 Duncan, for once, exerted himself to intervene. Bunny replied that it was not for Duncan to talk about seduction and morals like a Victorian father. But Duncan's concern was for Angelica, and the twenty-six-year difference in age. Bunny was not unnaturally stiffened in his resolve, however, and the encounter left Duncan angry, agitated and sleepless. But there was little more they could do, especially as further opposition would only encourage Angelica to agree to the marriage Bunny now proposed. It is a measure of the curious ambivalence felt by the participants in this struggle that Virginia was not told of the affair until May 1940. Her response was the same as her sister's. 'Pray God she [Angelica] may tire of that rusty surly slow old dog with his amorous ways and his primitive mind,' she wrote. It made her feel sadly old, with some of the emptiness that Vanessa surely felt, for the whole affair was without youth and laughter, and felt like a renewal of Julian's death. She hoped her niece would return in five weeks, repentant and wiser.

It was not to be. Angelica married Bunny, and had a quartet of daughters to continue the Bloomsbury line. Many years later she wrote a moving and perceptive autobiography, *Deceived with Kindness*. Subtitled 'A Bloomsbury Childhood', this exemplified the emotional honesty that the group admired, even if, as Leonard noted, they did not always practise it.

In 1941 Vanessa began work on her never-completed conversation piece depicting the members of the Memoir Club, which continued to meet irregularly. Duncan, Leonard, herself, Clive, Bunny, Maynard, Lydia, Desmond, Molly, Quentin and E. M. Forster were still alive, but on the wall hang portraits of Lytton, Roger and Virginia – all deceased members. For Virginia had drowned herself in the river near Rodmell earlier in the year.

She feared a return of insanity, recognizing the symptoms which had been held at bay for some twenty years, and also the very real possibility that Britain would be invaded by the forces of Nazi Germany, which had already occupied much of Europe. Leonard, as a socialist and a Jew, would have been an early casualty of such occupation. Vanessa, alerted by her sister's fears, had urged her to rest: 'what should I have done all these last 3 years if you hadn't been able to keep me alive and cheerful? You don't know how much I depend on you.' But Virginia was beyond the reach of argument or advice.

Her death seemed to herald the end of 'Bloomsbury', symbolically under-lined by the fact that so many of their homes and studios in London had already been destroyed by bombing in the early months of World War II. In all sorts of ways, these were darkened days.

In the aftermath of Julian's death, as Sandra Lummis has observed, Vanessa's painting acquired a thick, heavy impasto quite unlike her previous practice, and a sombre palette. [Picture 84] Though it would hardly be true to say that art proved a consolation, she continued to paint, using the new studio that had been made out of an attic at Charleston. [Picture 90] Here

One of the last photographs of Vanessa Bell.

Photograph of Virginia Woolf by Lettice Ramsay, 1932.

there was an accumulation of artists' objects – plaster busts, painted pots, printed fabrics and canvases stacked in the nearby roof space – and here, writes Richard Shone, Vanessa brought flowers and fruit from the garden. She painted many views from the window, and a series of self-portraits 'charting the transformation of her looks from care-worn middle-age to the shawled, bespectacled, resolute woman of eighty'.

She continued to get pleasure from Charleston, and from her grand-children. Quentin married Anne Olivier Popham, the daughter of very old acquaintances, and by a happy coincidence Angelica's daughter Henrietta married Burgo Partridge, son of Frances and Ralph. As her grandchildren grew up Vanessa played with and painted them.

Vanessa died in April 1961. Duncan's very last picture of her shows her at the easel in the garden room at Charleston that was also her bedroom, her hand poised as it approaches the canvas for what may stand for the last brushstroke, the final application of colour and line.

Clive ended his days in the company of Barbara Bagenal. When he died in 1956 the Memoir Club was formally wound up and 'Bloomsbury' may be said to have become a historical rather than living entity. Visiting Charleston again a few years later with Henrietta and her daughter Sophie (Vanessa's great-granddaughter) Frances noted in her diary what it all meant to her.

> Plunged in this old Bloomsbury civilization (for all we may have laughed at its 'croquet hoops' and the paint peeling here and there) I am overpowered with pleasure and emotion at the sense that all round me *real* values have been aimed at and achieved, and that the house, garden and all it contains is a unique work of art, something lovingly created and kept alive ... Even now when nearly all of them are dead, it is the same, and I have been struck by the fact that the feeling I have for it is partly gratitude ... One thing I am absolutely convinced of is that the lasting value of what Old Bloomsbury stood for and did will go on being recognized – indeed it *is* being recognized ...

One of Vanessa's last views of herself in the attic studio at Charleston may stand as a visual postscript to these words.

Vanessa Bell, *The Artist in her Studio*, 1952.
In 1938 this studio, with its large north-facing windows,
was created on the attic floor at Charleston for Vanessa's
use. Here she depicts herself surrounded by painter's
equipment – brushes, canvases, bottles of oil for
thinning and mixing colours.

SELECT BIBLIOGRAPHY

Further information on the lives and work of the Bloomsbury Group can be found in the following list of publications. In addition, both Charleston Farmhouse, Firle, Lewes, East Sussex, BN8 6LL and the home of Virginia Woolf, Monk's House, Rodmell, Lewes, BN7 3HF are open to the public. In London, the Bloomsbury Workshop, 12 Galen Place, WC1A 2FR offers a continuously changing stock of paintings, drawings, designs and books by and about Bloomsbury. Works by the Bloomsbury artists are also available from Sandra Lummis Fine Art, London, tel: 0181 340 2293.

Isabelle Anscombe, *Omega and After*, 1981
Anne Olivier Bell, ed. *The Diary of Virginia Woolf*, 5 vols, 1977–1984
Clive Bell, *Old Friends: Personal Recollections*, 1956
Quentin Bell, *Virginia Woolf: A Biography*, 1972
    Bloomsbury, 1974
Quentin Bell and Angelica Garnett, eds. *Vanessa Bell's Family Album*, 1981
Noel Carrington, *Carrington: Paintings, Drawings and Decorations*, 1980
Noel Carrington, ed. *Selected Letters of Mark Gertler*, 1965
Mary Ann Caws, *Women of Bloomsbury: Virginia, Vanessa and Carrington*, 1990
Hugh and Mirabel Cecil, *Clever Hearts: Desmond and Molly MacCarthy*, 1990
Charleston Trust, *Charleston Past and Present*, 1987
    see also *Charleston Magazine*, 1990 onwards
Judith Collins, *The Omega Workshop*, 1983
Sandra Darroch, *Ottoline: A Life of Lady Ottoline Morrell*, 1976
Louise DeSalvo and Mitchell Leaska, eds. *The Letters of Vita Sackville West to Virginia Woolf*, 1985
Roger Fry, *Vision and Design*, 1920
Angelica Garnett, *Deceived with Kindness*, 1984
David Garnett, *The Flowers of the Forest*, 1954
    The Familiar Faces, 1962
David Garnett, ed. *Dora Carrington: Letters and Extracts from her Diaries*, 1970
Robert Gathorne-Hardy, ed. *The Early Memoirs of Lady Ottoline Morrell*, 1963
    Ottoline at Garsington 1915–1918, 1974
Gretchen Gerzina, *Carrington: A Life*, 1989
Diane F. Gillespie, *The Sisters' Arts: the Writing and Painting of Virginia Woolf and Vanessa Bell*, 1988
Victoria Glendinning, *Vita: A Biography of Vita Sackville-West*, 1983
Nina Hamnett, *Laughing Torso: Reminiscences*, 1932
Jane Hill, *The Art of Dora Carrington*, 1994
Michael Holroyd, *Lytton Strachey*, 1994
Denise Hooker, *Nina Hamnett: Queen of Bohemia*, 1986
Richard Kennedy, *A Boy at the Hogarth Press*, 1972
Hugh Lee, ed. *A Cezanne in the Hedge*, 1992
John Lehmann, *Virginia Woolf*, 1975
    Thrown to the Woolfs, 1978
Desmond MacCarthy, *Memories*, 1953
Regina Marler, ed. *Selected Letters of Vanessa Bell*, 1993
John Middleton Murry, ed. *Katherine Mansfield's Letters to John Middleton Murry*, 1951
Gillian Naylor, ed. *Bloomsbury: Artists, Authors, Designers, by Themselves*, 1990

Nigel Nicolson, *Portrait of a Marriage*, 1973
Nigel Nicolson and Joanne Trautmann, eds. *The Letters of Virginia Woolf*, 1975–84
John Russell Noble, ed. *Recollections of Virginia Woolf*, 1972
Vincent O'Sullivan, ed. *Selected Letters of Katherine Mansfield*, 1989
Frances Partridge, *A Pacifist's War*, 1978
    Julia, 1979
    Memories, 1981
    Friends in Focus: A Life in Photographs, 1987
Richard Shone, *Bloomsbury Portraits*, second edition, 1993
Miranda Seymour, *Ottoline Morrell*, 1992
Frances Spalding, *Roger Fry*, 1980
    Vanessa Bell, 1983
    ed. *Virginia Woolf: Paper Darts*, 1991
Frederick Spotts, ed. *Letters of Leonard Woolf*, 1975–80
Denys Sutton, ed. *Letters of Roger Fry*, 1972
Claire Tomalin, *Katherine Mansfield*, 1988
Simon Watney, *English Post-Impressionism*, 1980
    The Art of Duncan Grant, 1990
John Woodeson, *Mark Gertler*, 1972
Leonard Woolf, *Beginning Again: An Autobiography of the Years 1911–1918*, 1964
    Downhill All the Way: 1919–1939, 1967
Virginia Woolf, *Roger Fry: A Biography*, 1940
    The Complete Shorter Fiction, 1989
    see also *Collected Works*

PICTURE CREDITS